The Imagined, the Imag

The Imagined, the Imaginary and the Symbolic

Maurice Godelier

Translated by Nora Scott

VERSO

London • New York

This work was published with the help of the French
Ministry of Culture – Centre national du livre

Ouvrage publié avec le concours du Ministère français
chargé de la Culture–Centre national du livre

This English-language edition published by Verso 2020
Originally published in French as *L'Imaginé, l'imaginaire & le symbolique*
© CNRS Editions 2015
Translation © Nora Scott 2020

1 3 5 7 9 10 8 6 4 2

Verso
UK: 6 Meard Street, London W1F 0EG
US: 20 Jay Street, Suite 1010, Brooklyn, NY 11201
versobooks.com

Verso is the imprint of New Left Books

ISBN-13: 978-1-78663-770-3
ISBN-13: 978-1-78663-768-0 (LIBRARY)
ISBN-13: 978-1-78663-772-7 (UK EBK)
ISBN-13: 978-1-78663-771-0 (US EBK)

British Library Cataloguing in Publication Data
A catalogue record for this book is available from the British Library

Library of Congress Cataloging-in-Publication Data
A catalog record for this book is available from the Library of Congress

Typeset in Minion Pro by Hewer Text UK Ltd, Edinburgh
Printed and bound by CPI Group (UK) Ltd, Croydon CR0 4YY

For Lina and Zacharias,
And in memory of the immense scholar,
and my good friend, Jack Goody.

Contents

Foreword

Why this book, and why this title? In the first place, because not everything that is imagined is imaginary. And since everything that is imagined is done so by the mind, we must analyse how and why, in certain domains, the mind produces imagined content that is imaginary and, in other domains, imagined content that is not. In his two books *The Imagination* and *The Imaginary*, Jean-Paul Sartre did not make this distinction, yet it is a strategic one.[1]

We all know, from daily experience, that we can be at the same time present in the moment by our consciousness but absent by our mind, even though consciousness is also mind. And we also know that when our mind projects itself beyond the present, it is not the same thing to represent to ourselves facts that no longer exist but did exist at one time, such as scenes from our childhood, as it is facts that do not yet exist but will exist in the future, such as a planned vacation to Istanbul; or facts that can never exist but which we can imagine, such as the invasion of the earth by giant spiders from a planet billions of light years away.

There are several kinds of imaginaries, and our relations with each of them, therefore, cannot be the same. To obtain a clearer picture, let us make a very short – all too short – inventory; as we will see, the distinctions between these imaginaries always seem to emerge

---

1 In *The Imagination*, trans. K. Williford, D. Rudrauf (London: Routledge, 2012 [1936]), Sartre is chiefly, and rightly, concerned to show that our 'mental images' are not 'in' the mind but are part of the mind. In *The Imaginary: A Phenomenological Study of the Imagination*, trans. J. Webber (London: Routledge, 2004 [1940]), having shown that 'the function of imagining' should be described as a 'constituent structure of the consciousness essence' and analysed how an actor 'unrealizes himself' in the character of Hamlet, or the reader of a novel in the book's hero, Sartre concludes that the imagination is the conscious mind as a whole, insofar as it realises its freedom and reveals both the creation and the annihilation of the world. Oddly enough, Sartre does not allude to the religious imaginary or to that of political systems, which are anything but negligible in our being.

from the singular relationship each entertains with the 'real'. Which raises the inevitable question: What is the real?

Take play, keeping in mind that all children the world over have played, and that once they are adults many continue to play in other forms. The child playing cowboys and brandishing noisy revolvers that cannot kill knows that he (is and) is not a 'real' cowboy. And, when he was younger and scolded his teddy bear for having wet on the carpet, he already knew that Teddy was not a 'real' bear and had not 'really' wet on the carpet.

Or take the arts, and the example of the *Iliad* and the *Odyssey*, which since antiquity have been attributed to the great poet Homer. Perhaps Homer was not the only author of these masterworks, but neither was he Achilles or Ulysses, whose feats he sang. And perhaps neither Ulysses nor Achilles ever 'really' existed, either, but we thrill to the tale of the many dangers Ulysses faced, threatened with the deadly grip of the Cyclops or the loving embrace of Circe as, after the fall of Troy, he sailed towards Ithaca where his faithful wife, Penelope, had been waiting for years.

We do not expect poets or their work to depict historical events as they happened. Furthermore, are not historical events perhaps also a mixture of the real and the imaginary? When inscriptions or monuments dating back several thousands of years tell us that the Babylonian king Nebuchadnezzar II (605–552 BCE), after conquering the Egyptians and subjugating the kings of all the major cities of Syria and Arabia, as well as the king of Judah after taking Jerusalem (597), proclaimed himself King of Kings and decreed that the god Marduk, with whom he had made a pact and who had led him from victory to victory, was the paramount god,[2] what is a professional historian to do with these real events that rest on belief in the existence of imaginary beings and worlds?

Here we have a paradox. If Nebuchadnezzar II really believed that the god Marduk had led him from victory to victory, we find ourselves

---

2 Having learned of his father's death while he was away at war, Nebuchadnezzar II returned to Babylon to touch the hand of the statue of Marduk in his temple and receive from him the throne of the kingdom.

in the domain of religious beliefs and forms of political power associated, or even fused with, one religion or another. The paradox, then, is that the imaginary that underpins and informs these religions and forms of power is never conceived or experienced as imaginary by those who believe. On the contrary, this imaginary is conceived and experienced as even more real than the realities people experience in their daily lives. That particular imaginary, more real than the real, is superreal, surreal. But once again, what is the real? And could we espouse Lévi-Strauss's threefold affirmation that in myth, 'the real, the symbolic and the imaginary' are 'three separate categories'?[3] This may be true of myths – and we will return to the question – but it is no longer true when it comes to ritual, sacred objects, temples, et cetera, which clearly attest to the reality, and therefore to the truth, that gods or God exist, not to mention spirits and ancestors. And everything that attests to this truth is at the same time the symbol of this truth. Once again, we find ourselves in the realms of belief and of the symbolic, which plays a paramount role in believing. How, then, are we to distinguish the real from the symbolic, or the imaginary from the symbolic? Might symbols be more real than what they symbolise?[4] But what is the symbolic, and can it help us distinguish the real from the imaginary? Perhaps not, if the symbolic function is a prior condition for any form of activity and thought that has meaning for people. This is because the symbolic function is the wellspring of all possible forms of signifiers, which enable humans to signify as much what they think and do as what they are unwilling or unable to think or do.

The symbolic thus extends beyond thought and the mind to fill and mobilise the entire body, its gaze, gestures, postures, as well as everything that projects outside individuals the meanings they have

---

3   C. Lévi-Strauss, *The Origin of Table Manners*, Mythologiques, vol. 3, trans. J. and D. Weightman (Chicago: University of Chicago Press, 1990), 84–85. In a lecture planned for 8 July 1953 in Rome, but which in fact was never given, Lacan, too, spoke of the 'three quite *distinct* levels which are the essential levels of human reality and which are called the symbolic, the imaginary and the real'. See J. Lacan, *Des noms du père* (Paris: Le Seuil, 2005), 12.

4   C. Lévi-Strauss, *Introduction to the Work of Marcel Mauss*, trans. F. Baker (London: Routledge & Kegan Paul, 1987), 37.

given to the world – temples, palaces, tools, foods, mountains, the sea, the sky and the earth – as they think and feel them.

Of course, language is at the heart of the symbolic function since words are symbols and designate that which is not themselves. But language is not the whole of the symbolic and does not exhaust it. If the symbolic is present in every form of activity or thought, then symbols cannot have the same content or play the same role in mathematics, art and religion. And, it seems that when symbols are invented for the purposes of religious beliefs, some of them change their nature and undergo a veritable transmutation. Once masks, icons, sacramental formulae, and so on have become sacred objects, they seem also to contain in themselves the invisible beings they designate. It is as though these invisible beings appropriate for their own purposes the symbols people have made in order to communicate with them and to bid their presence. These are the areas we will attempt to explore and steps we will follow to do so.

A final word: it should be remembered that, as an anthropologist, I will be analysing primarily imaginaries that are 'shared' by the members of a given society or the followers of a religion.

Some Points of Reference

To inquire into the nature and role of the imaginary and the symbolic is to attempt to account for the basic components of all societies. But because the two are connected, it is also to attempt to explain the essential aspects of the human way of life, aspects which, in every instance, form a large portion of the social and private parts of our identity. To shed some light on our endeavour, I will cite a few examples of imaginary and symbolic material that form part of the social fabric and the way of life of those living in a society, while stressing that such a list, however long, can never be complete.

The worlds that spring from the imaginary are, first of all, the founding myths of religions, or those that have legitimised political systems or other power regimes that have emerged throughout history. Two examples: the Chinese notion of the Mandate of Heaven, which legitimised one man's right to become emperor; or that of the God-given right invoked by the Catholic king Louis XIV in exercising his absolute power over his kingdom's subjects. But in addition to religions and political systems, we should not forget that there are many other social relations built on an imaginary component.

The assertions that humans 'descend' from each other either solely through men or solely through women are two purely imaginary postulates, each of which acts as a departure point and mental framework for the formation of kin groups organised according to a patrilineal or a matrilineal descent rule. We find ourselves here at the heart of kinship, with the full consequences of these imaginary postulates weighing, for instance, on the asserted or denied role of semen or menstrual blood in making children. The same postulates justify the appropriation of offspring of unions between members of these societies by adults, who have different rights and duties with regard to these children according to whether they are maternal or paternal kin.

In fact, there can be no religion, power system, kinship system or other social relations without the support and effectiveness of numerous symbolic components that not only express the nature of these relations but cause them to exist socially, collectively, and within the mind and body of all those who must reproduce them daily through their acts and works. For religions, these symbolic elements include rites, places of worship – totemic sites, mosques, temples, sacred mountains, et cetera – as well as offerings, sacrifices, prayers, invocations, chants, songs, dances, and attitudes and gestures, whether prescribed (prostration, genuflection) or proscribed (blasphemy), concerning the gods, spirits and ancestors. In the case of political systems, we can mention palaces; fortresses; big, chiefly houses; sceptres; thrones; insignia of rank within military or administrative hierarchies; and commemorations of moments that founded a new society (for the French, the storming of the Bastille on 14 July 1789 and the song 'La Marseillaise', which became the national anthem).

However, the distinction between religion and politics is recent in the history of humankind and present in only a few societies. For thousands of years, religion and politics were inseparable and even fused. Jupiter was Rome's first citizen (*primus civis*). The Chinese emperor, the Wang, was 'the Unique Man', the only one capable of uniting Heaven and Earth (the components of the character Wang), and therefore the only one qualified to celebrate the great cosmic rituals for the benefit of the peoples of the Empire.

The *tu'i tonga*, or Polynesian paramount chief, whose power was said to extend over a hundred islands in the middle of the Pacific Ocean, claimed to descend directly from Tangaloa, one of the major gods in the Polynesian pantheon, who had infused into the chief's body a component of his divine force – the most powerful 'mana', which no other man could possess. As a consequence, when the tu'i tonga celebrated the rites of the passage of seasons, his mana was believed to make the women's wombs fertile and multiply the riches of the sea and the land.

In order for these ancestors, spirits and gods, normally invisible to the human eye, to become present when not incarnated in the body of a man or a woman, carvings, paintings and masks would lend them form and matter. Did not the goddess Athena, patron of Athens, dwell in the Parthenon in a body sculpted by Phidias in the fifth century BCE? Did not Johann Sebastian Bach put his talent to work composing the *Saint Matthew Passion* (1729) and El Greco his to painting *The Holy Trinity* (1577) on the altar screen of the Monastery of Saint Dominic in Toledo? And, countless works of art have been dedicated to glorifying the power of the powerful among men; I will choose only one, the *Portrait of Louis XIV*, painted by Rigaud in 1701, a theological-political representation of the king of France as 'absolute' monarch.

But imaginary and symbolic creations are by no means the monopoly of religious and political systems, of kinship systems or of any other social relationship that gives rise to a collective identity and practices that must be manifested and celebrated. They pervade the even-larger domain of artistic works and practices that are meant, above all, to express the personality and inner life of their creators; to express their dreams, their emotions, their anger and their hopes: whether it is Goya's *The Nude Maja* (ca. 1797), or Picasso's *Guernica* (1937), which proclaims his horror and pain at the massacres committed by Franco's troops and their German allies during the Spanish Civil War.

And can we forget the novelists, poets, songwriters, playwrights and filmmakers who transport us to worlds that exist only in and through their works? The French poet Paul Verlaine's famous alliterations, 'les sanglots longs des violons de l'automne bercent mon coeur d'une langueur monotone' [the long sobbing of the violins of autumn lull my heart with monotonous languor], reproduce the sound of the long sobbing notes of the violins of autumn. Although everyone knows that the violins of autumn and their sobbing notes have never existed – that they are metaphors, figures of speech – the images and music of these words can inspire feelings in us that suggest the smell of rain and dead leaves associated with the word 'autumn'. But metaphors are not only the matter of myth or poetry; everyday language is full of them as well. We will return to this. Finally, how could I fail to mention fairy tales – *Snow White and the Seven Dwarves* – illustrated books for children, but also for adults – Mickey Mouse, *Tintin and the Temple of the Sun*, Tarzan, Japanese manga – and, of course, games – cards, chess, ball games, and so on: play invites the players temporarily into a virtual world that they themselves create when they play by the rules invented so they may confront each other (and have fun doing it). But the game world vanishes as soon as the game is over.

To bring to an end a list that has no possible end, I will mention those symbolic objects par excellence: toys, dolls, stuffed bears, Batman costumes, plastic Kalashnikovs, et cetera. Through them, children multiply their 'selves' and explore the imagined and imaginary worlds they have invented, and they do this without ever leaving their room, their apartment or their parents' garden. Reading this list, one may get the idea that human existence is nothing more than imaginary and symbolic realities. This is by no means the case, but even so, there are men and women who believe they are Napoleon or Joan of Arc. The imaginary seems to have taken them over, and because of this they are no longer able to live like, or with, other people. An effort must, then, be made to make them aware that they are not who or what they imagine themselves to be, that they are 'really' someone else, an other. But they can persist in denying or refusing this other within themselves, which is their initial ego. Could Don Quixote, who was not 'completely' mad, hear the warnings of Sancho Panza, his valet whom he saw as his squire, when he said that the knights he was challenging or preparing to fight were merely windmills? Is there something in addition to the imaginary and the symbolic that, together with them, makes up human reality? What is the nature of this additional component? And what relationship does it entertain with the imaginary and the symbolic? Are these relations of complementarity or opposition? Or of mutual exclusion? To answer these questions, we will have to analyse what is meant by the words 'imagine', 'symbolise', 'believe', 'possible', 'impossible', 'unbelievable', 'real', and so on.

But before getting down to this subject, I must warn the reader that the present book will not be dealing with the 'imaginary self' that each of us constructs, unaware that this part of ourselves is imaginary.[5] Nor will I examine Lacan's three fathers hovering over each of us: the 'real' father we have, the 'imaginary' father we would like to have had, and the 'symbolic' father who is the father of no one in particular but is the embodiment, for everyone, of the inner presence of the law that presides over desire, the exercise of our sexuality. These imaginaries are always singular, attesting to a particular life story, but one in which the analyst can decipher the effects of universal unconscious processes.[6] These imaginaries that structure the ego but elude its conscious awareness are often the symptoms and symbols of a difficulty in living, a suffering, of which some ask an analyst to help them to become aware and distance themselves.[7]

Exploring this domain is not the job of anthropologists, however, but the work of psychologists, psychiatrists and psychoanalysts. As an anthropologist, I will investigate other imaginaries: those of games and of art, where the distinction between what is imaginary and what is not is conscious and experienced; those of the founding myths of religious and political systems, which are shared and believed to be given by the gods, God or reason, but which are not experienced and recognised as imaginary. On the contrary, these are held to be the invisible but ever-present basis of reality, a surreal portion of the real.

---

5 J. Lacan, *On the Names-of-the-Father*, trans. B. Fink (Cambridge: Polity, 2013): 'We must absolutely define the ego's imaginary function as the unity of the subject who is alienated from himself. The ego is something in which the subject cannot recognize himself at first except by alienating himself' (24).

6 Ibid., 24.

7 Ibid. 'The analyst is the ... symbol of omnipotence ... Seeking him out, the patient adopts a certain stance which is approximately as follows: "You're the one who possesses my truth." This stance is completely illusory, but it is the typical stance' (35). And on p. 38: 'The analyst comes to symbolize the superego, which is the symbol of symbols. The superego is simply speech [*une parole*] that says nothing.'

Of course, I have often talked with psychoanalysts about the nature and the basis of the hetero- and homosexual incest taboos, as well as about the defining characteristics of human sexuality. I have defined the latter as polymorphous (it is homo- and heterosexual); polytropic (the sexual drive does not distinguish spontaneously between permitted and prohibited persons); generalised, because it is present throughout the body; and cerebralised – in other words it functions as much in reaction to internal representations as it does to external stimuli and results in the disjunction between sexuality-as-desire (pleasure) and sexuality-as-reproduction. But everywhere, sexuality, which is in itself a-social, is placed in the service of and subordinated to the reproduction of social relations and issues which go beyond it and make it into a ventriloquist's dummy, obliged to testify in favour of the legitimacy or illegitimacy of a social order that encompasses and traverses it.[8]

---

8 M. Godelier and J. Hassoun, eds, *Meurtre du Père, Sacrifice de la sexualité. Approches anthropologiques et psychanalytiques* (Strasbourg: Éditions Arcanes, 1996); and M. Godelier, *Metamorphoses of Kinship*, trans. N. Scott (London and New York: Verso, 2012), chaps. 11, 12 on the origin and basis of the incest taboo.

Part I

From the Real to the Unreal

CHAPTER ONE

Concerning a Few Invariants

I will begin by recalling a few self-evident truths about human nature, in other words, a few invariants encountered at all times in history and in all forms of society:

- A human being is an individual – a man or a woman – who is not at the origin of him- or herself but is born of a man and a woman in another generation and from whom he or she has inherited his or her body.[1]
- He or she is an individual who, during the first years of life, cannot survive without the care and protection of other humans, adults capable of providing these and acknowledging a duty to do so.
- He or she is an individual born in a society they have not chosen, and which precedes them and in all likelihood those who gave birth to them.
- He or she is an individual with the capacity to learn and speak a language and who begins by learning the language spoken to them (before and) after their birth. They did not invent or choose this language any more than did those who speak it to them, and they share this language with the other members of the society to which they all belong.

Do not misunderstand me here. Human nature is, indissolubly, at the same time biological, social and cultural; none of these elements ever exist alone but are always shaped and transformed by the other two. At the outset, each human being possesses a bodily and sexual identity that situates them with respect to others and to him- or herself. And this is true even if the person suffers from and rejects the sexual

---

1   Medical progress today enables 'surrogate' mothers to bear a child made by two women and a man.

identity attributed to them by their body and by others, as is the case for transsexuals. Because a penis or a vagina is a part of their body, human beings find themselves assigned a social representation, whether or not they have chosen it, which transforms their sexual identity into a gender, which is male or female. Once this happens, each person, according to their gender, will occupy a different place and status in their society with respect to the other gender, with the consequence that they have different and unequal access to the political and religious functions necessary to the perpetuation of their society.

Whatever the nature of the social relations an individual entertains with others, these relations exist on two planes. They exist at once *between* individuals and *inside* each one, but do so in different ways depending on the place each person occupies in these relations. If, for example, a society has some form of marriage to make official and legitimate the union and the life shared by two individuals of different sex, a person cannot get married without knowing the meaning of marriage and who it is possible or impossible to marry, with respect to the taboo on incest and the prohibitions attached to belonging to a caste, a class, a profession, a religion, and so on. All social relations thus exist in a form that is both intersubjective and subjective, immaterial and material, corporeal and mental. By 'mental' [*idéel* in French] I mean the whole set of representations a society shares about the nature and origin of an institution, marriage for instance, as well as the prescriptions and proscriptions necessary to its implementation, to which must be added the emotions induced by this implementation, all of which depend on each person's gender and intimate life history.

It is this fundamentally anthropological perspective that reveals the meaning of the fourfold dependence which provides the invariable framework of human nature. Let us reconsider it from this standpoint. All humans are born from the sexual union of a man and a woman, but depending on the rule governing descent in the society into which they are born, an individual will belong to their father's group if the kinship system is patrilineal, or to their mother's group if the system is matrilineal, or to both groups but in different ways if the system is bilineal or undifferentiated.

Whether the person 'descends' only through men, or only through women, or through both is each time an imaginary social and cultural postulate which entails a whole series of diverging consequences for the constitution of kin groups, clans, lineages and houses, the construction of which is based on this postulate. But it also conditions the representations of men and women in making a baby; the role of semen or menstrual blood; the role of the ancestors or the gods, or God, in transforming the foetus into a child; the name it will be given; and more.[2] In addition, if it is necessary to contract alliances with others in order to produce offspring, it is because a person cannot, without committing incest, marry within their own group someone who is socially and culturally defined and forbidden by the society. And, if sexuality must be subject to social prohibitions, it is because, in its spontaneous state, as a biological drive and need, human sexuality is a-social (not anti-social).

To be sure, kinship relations – whether this kinship is 'real', adoptive, or of some other nature – play a fundamental role in the first years and stages of our subjective and social construction; nevertheless, there is no such thing as a kin-based society. The only human relations capable of making a society are those that establish and legitimise the sovereignty of social groups created by kinship, class or other factors over a territory, its inhabitants and its resources. These are what in the West are called political-religious relations. And everywhere such relations encompass, crosscut and subordinate kin groups and their relations to their own reproduction.

Lastly, even if an individual never chooses the society into which they are born, or the social status of those who gave birth to or adopted them, this social status attaches to them at birth, and depending on the society, the epoch and their personal history, they may or may not

---

2   Contrary to Lévi-Strauss's affirmation, descent is not on the side of nature and alliance on the side of culture. The forms of descent are just as much culturally defined as are the forms of alliance. See M. Godelier, *Lévi-Strauss*, trans. N. Scott (London and New York: Verso, 2018), 104, 115.

be able or desire to keep, change or reject the status to which they were born. A Brahmin's son will become a Brahmin and must marry a woman from his caste (*jati*) on pain of becoming an outcaste.

It is by learning to understand and then to speak the language spoken to them since birth in the interactions with those who surround and care for them that a person consciously and unconsciously absorbs the norms that organise the shared life of their society, together with the attached representations and values that express them.

By now, we already suspect that such a being, born under this fourfold dependency, can be neither an 'absolute subject' nor a 'transcendental subject', even if philosophers may imagine or think this is the case. But some kind of subject they must be, since in order to live they must act, and to act they must be conscious of their own existence, of the existence of the other humans that interact with them and of that of the surrounding world. To be conscious is to think, but thinking is more than being conscious, since some operations of the mind are unconscious and because thought can never be present at its own birth in each of us.

So, here we are, back at the intersection of the problems that arise when we try to define the meaning of words such as the *imaginary*, the *symbolic* or the *real*. For if imagining is a faculty of the mind and a conscious act, we must then explain the fact that not everything that is imagined is imaginary. What is the difference between the imaginary imagined and the imagined that is not? Is the imagined that is not imaginary the same as the 'real'? Or, since the products of the imagination are representations (associated with emotions), does the non-imaginary imagined correspond to all those representations of a non-imaginary real? Perhaps. But there are also many imaginary realities that are neither thought nor experienced as imaginary, but as more 'real' than the visible real, as *surreal*; these are imaginary realities such as religions, their rites, their celebrants, their places of worship.

Another example, taken from the news, is that of the present possibility of asking a 'surrogate' mother to carry a baby. Whereas for thousands of years, the birth of a child implied that a woman became pregnant, carried her child in her womb for nine months (if the child was full term), and gave birth, it is now possible for a woman who has had repeated miscarriages and still desires a child to allow one of her eggs, fertilised by her companion or spouse, to be transferred into the body of another woman who will ensure the child's gestation and birth. However, when the child is born, it will not belong to the surrogate mother, but to the man and woman who conceived it and to whom it will be genetically and socially connected in the same way (ideally) as a child in a 'traditional' Western monogamous family. What used to be a single biological process in which fertilisation, pregnancy and birth succeeded each other in the body of one woman can now be broken down into two phases and carried out by two women in no way related to each other.

Moreover, it is only with the help of symbolic props that the imagined, whether imaginary or not, can exist, be communicated and take on a social existence. Of course, among these props we find language. But the same word, such as 'coyote', does not mean the same thing when used in everyday language as it does in that of myth. The literal sense would correspond to the 'real world' coyote, and the figurative meaning to the coyote of the imaginary world of mythology. But, would an Indian perceive the two meanings as being opposed, mutually exclusive, or rather as complementary, designating and describing two aspects of the animal that hunted, like they did, on the Great Plains of North America? Beyond language and words, there are other means of transforming the imaginary into social and material realities, for example, masks, statues, body painting, and so forth. To be sure. However, in Europe carnival masks only conceal men and women whose identities will be discovered later, while in the case of the masks of the Sulka, a tribe in New Britain, in Oceania, admired by André Breton for their splendour, the wearers' identity must never be revealed. Made over a period of months in the secret recesses of the forest, far from the eyes of women and noninitiates, their original forms, their huge size, their vibrant colours had no purpose other than to attract the spirits of the ancestors or other entities so that they might manifest their presence when the mask wearers danced onto the village meeting ground. Before the awed and terrified eyes of those who discovered them at that moment, the spirit masks would perform sometimes for only a few minutes before once again vanishing into the forest to be thrown into the bush and left to decompose.[3] But here we are already talking about the imaginary in art. Let us come back, for the moment, to the conscious mind, since it is the primary source of the realities that concern us: the imagined, the imaginary and the symbolic.

---

3 M. Jeudy-Ballini, 'Dédommager le désir. Le prix de l'émotion en Nouvelle-Bretagne', Terrain 32 (1999), 5–20.

CHAPTER TWO

Consciousness and the Mind

To be conscious is always to be conscious of something. There is no such thing as empty consciousness.[1] And everything of which the conscious mind is conscious means something to it. Consciousness is therefore also thought. It is an act of the mind, which at the same time attaches meaning, significations, to the things targeted by consciousness. So consciousness is that whereby the thinking of an individual, of a subject (whom we will call *ego*), directs itself mentally towards an 'object', whatever it may be. This 'object' can be information provided by the person's own body, internal sensations; it can be the perception of an object or a set of objects outside the self; it can be the desire to paint or to answer a phone call; and so on. Consciousness is thus a continuous series of acts aimed at objects which each time take on 'meaning' for the conscious mind. The intentionality of the conscious mind has nothing to do with the intentions an individual may have to do or not do something. The intentionality of the conscious mind is the act whereby the mind defines and operates the meaning of the object viewed as a concrete object, or as a mathematical ideality, or as an imaginary world, or as a relation between things or people, and so on.

'Meaning' exists only for a conscious mind; the only meaning is that given, produced by the mind. There is no such thing as an isolated intentionality, for a targeted 'object' is always part of an encompassing whole. We do not listen to Beethoven's Fifth Symphony note by note. Likewise, the meaning of a sentence remains present, even as it is continually modified, until the sentence has been uttered in its entirety. The individual (ego) exists not only as a singular body, but

---

1   E. Husserl, *Ideas Pertaining to a Pure Phenomenology and to a Phenomenological Philosophy – Book I: General Introduction to a Pure Phenomenology*, trans. F. Kersten (The Hague: Nijhoff, 1982 [1913]), 63, 131.

also as the subject of all the intentional, conscious acts he or she performs simultaneously and successively.[2] He or she exists as the centre from which these continuous acts emanate and as the place to which all experiences, ideas, emotions and desires associated with the individual's conscious mind belong. In short, ego exists as a body, as thought and as subjectivity.

Therefore, if we are to perceive the faculties of the conscious mind, we must take a closer look at its structures. The conscious mind is conscious of itself. Sartre called the fact that it knows it exists 'the great ontological law' of consciousness.[3] Ego's consciousness is always already inhabited, even before birth, by the presence of the world around it: a specific natural environment, society, culture and language, and a particular time in history. Consciousness is also the internal consciousness of time. This consciousness exists in the present, but to this present are always attached elements of the recent past and the imminent future. But the conscious mind can also step back from the present the subject is living and from the world with which he or she is involved. It can represent to itself past events that once existed but no longer do. It can represent to itself future events whose realisation seems unlikely for the time being. We see clearly that if the 'things' that present themselves to the conscious mind have meaning for it, it is because the mind gives or has given them this meaning. It is by thought that consciousness can be both present in the present and, at the same time, make real or imaginary events retrieved from the past or projected into the future present by their absence. In short, the conscious mind has the capacity to step back from the experienced present while remaining present to it; and this faculty comes from the fact that the human mind can 'imagine'.

More than a property, then, it is the very essence of the mind to be able to examine itself and to step back from its content. Reflexivity is constituent of consciousness. It is already present in ordinary,

---

2   Ibid., 100ff, 113.

3   J.-P. Sartre, *The Imagination*: 'The sole manner of existing for a consciousness is in having consciousness that it exists' (113).

spontaneous awareness, since to be aware of something particular is both to target and to highlight this thing against the backdrop of underlying consciousness. And this highlighting immediately establishes a distance between consciousness and what it has highlighted. This is the first degree of conscious reflexivity.

But there is a second degree, which appears when the mind inquires into the nature of that of which it is conscious. The way, then, is opened to an attempt to understand the nature of the relations surrounding the subject: relations between things perceived, relations between other interacting humans, but also those between these humans and things. In this search for meaning, it is the subject that reveals and discovers itself, and that positions itself with respect to others and to things. The second degree of reflexivity available to consciousness opens the way to knowledge, art and the invention of religions, but also to the production of concrete skills.

Nevertheless, there is a fundamental constituent of consciousness I have not yet talked about, and without which we cannot understand the forms of reflexivity available to the conscious mind, nor the subject's capacity to understand the world around them and their place, their identity within this world. The missing component is language. Language is immanent to consciousness and inseparable from thought. Before going into the analysis of language, however, it must be clarified that some thought processes are not conscious, but instead either underlie the operations of the mind (the rules of grammar of a language, for example), or belong to the deeper layers of the unconscious part of thinking. This clarification is fundamental because it precludes reducing our knowledge of the nature of the mind merely to the processes of which it is aware. The unconscious mind also contributes to the production of meaning, the meanings the mind gives to the world. We must not forget this.

CHAPTER THREE

Language and the Mind

To analyse the relationship between the mind and language, we will start from what linguists and psychologists have taught us about the mechanisms and stages of language acquisition in children. How do children come, first, to understand, then, to speak the language spoken to and around them before and since their birth? Speech cannot be dissociated from language. It is its accomplishment. Language is at once a means of communication with others and a means of action on others and on oneself. The great apes also possess complex systems of visual, gestural and vocal communication, but they do not have spoken language. However, all languages spoken by humans presuppose these capacities. To explore these questions, we are going to leave phenomenology and turn to linguistics and psychology.

In 1975, the linguist Noam Chomsky showed that language acquisition could not be explained, as it was at the time, simply as a result of imitation and learning.[1] To account for the rapidity, the regularity of the stages and the relative independence of this acquisition from differences in children's intelligence and social context, we must therefore posit the existence of a universal mechanism inscribed in the genetic heritage of humankind and therefore in the brain of every child born. And it is this mechanism that enables the child to extract the model of language from that spoken by the adults, and to reproduce it.

It was during the biosocial evolution of our ancestors, sometime between *Homo habilis* and *Homo sapiens*, that the capacity to learn a spoken language became inscribed in our genetic code and thus

---

1 N. Chomsky, *Syntactic Structures* (The Hague: Mouton, 1957); *Language and Mind* (Cambridge: Cambridge University Press, 2006 [1968]).

possessed its own neural base.[2] Several conditions must be present in order for a child to understand the language spoken to it and to speak it. It must be able to distinguish 'linguistically relevant' sounds from among all the sounds it hears. Then, it must be able to cut up the flow of words addressed to it or which it hears, and to classify them according to their meaning. Finally, one day, the child will recognise in the adults' speech their intention to signify.

But language is not the only means of self-expression and communication among humans. The whole body participates, through the gaze, gestures, facial expressions, cries, signs, and so on. As we will see, all these forms of communication are aspects of the symbolising function, which is also inscribed in the human mind. Even before birth, the child is already familiar with the voice of the woman carrying it in her womb, and with the sounds of the language she speaks. After birth, the infant will be immersed in a world of sounds, smells, handling of its body, words spoken to it, all of which inform it about the surrounding world. The child will seek to communicate with this world via its gaze, through a repertory of facial expressions and gestures used to show pleasure, fear, well-being, distress and so on. In short, if the child needs others to survive, it already seeks also to communicate with others by bodily means. Later, when the infant becomes a baby, it will babble and play with the sounds produced. Between nine and eighteen months of age, it will gradually discover the meaning of the words spoken to it, even before it can actually pronounce them. This means that children must start by understanding, to a certain extent, what is going on around them and within them before they can choose the words to talk about it. The connection between the appropriate word and cognition is therefore clear, even if there is a time lag between being able to understand words and being able to produce them.[3]

---

2   B. de Boysson-Bardies, *Comment la parole vient aux enfants* (Paris: Odile Jacob, 1996), 14.

3   Ibid., 163.

And then, between eighteen and twenty-four months, when the child has come to understand what others are saying, it will quickly start talking. Let us not forget that, in order to produce the sounds of articulated speech, there must be a vocal tract that makes it possible. And the vocal tract of the infant does not allow it to do this. In the months following birth, we see a reconfiguration of the organs that will allow the child to speak. It will be helped by the gaze, gestures, the voice, by dialogues with those taking care of it. Once the baby becomes a young child, in order to speak the language spoken to it, it will have to associate sounds and meaning according to phonological and syntactical rules, to the rhythm and the intonation of a particular language. The bulk of the grammar of this language will thus be internalised and acquired before anyone teaches it to the child.[4] Yet it is not until the age of six that it will master more or less completely the pronunciation and grammar of its language.

Understanding a language obviously means understanding the words strung together into a sentence. Which raises the question: What is a word? A word is a linguistic sign, but it is two things at once. From the standpoint of morphology, it is a combination of sounds that correspond to the phonological forms characteristic of each language, a 'semantic unit' linked to its 'vocal space'. From the standpoint of meaning, a word is an ideality, a symbol.[5] It is, according to Saussure's famous formula, the inseparable unit of signifier (sounds) and signified (meaning),[6] and, as he often repeated, the defining characteristic of human language is the arbitrary character[7] of the signifier with respect to the signified. There is no resemblance between the French 'vache', the English 'cow' and the animal these words

---

4 Ibid., 218.

5 Ibid., 139.

6 F. de Saussure, *Course in General Linguistics*, ed. C. Bally and A. Sechehaye in collab. with A. Riedlinger, trans. W. Baskin (New York: McGraw-Hill, 1915).

7 Ibid. 'The word *arbitrary* also calls for comment. The term should not imply that the choice of the signifier is left entirely to the speaker (we shall see below that the individual does not have the power to change a sign in any way once it has become established in the linguistic community; I mean that it is unmotivated, i.e., arbitrary in that it actually has no natural connection with the signified' (68–69).

designate. This absence of resemblance and the non-motivated nature of the signifier mean that words are 'symbols', according to the classification of signs developed by C. S. Peirce. A word is therefore neither a simple signal nor an icon. We will return to this point.

But in order to recognise a word, a mental representation must be produced that corresponds to this word which is a sound pattern. Thus, the representation must posit as equivalent the various ways of pronouncing the same word ('dog', for instance) that the child hears, whoever pronounces or has pronounced it and in whatever context. The equivalence the child establishes among all the ways the same word is pronounced makes the mental representation of this word a schematic mental reality, with an abstract pattern and an individualised ideality. Of course, the child is not aware of the unconscious mental operations involved in establishing the equivalence of ways of pronouncing and using a word.

In learning to recognise the meaning of the words and phrases spoken to or around them, and then learning to say them, children unconsciously reactivate the significations their society and culture have given these words. The words and their uses divide the world up into categories based on the child's experiences. These categories distinguish inanimate objects belonging to the realm of nature (rocks, rain, sun, etc.), culture (ball, doll, bicycle, etc.), persons (father, mother, big sister, etc.), situations (being in bed, falling down, etc.), actions (playing, eating, running, etc.) and interactions between and with persons.[8]

Acquiring 'vocabulary', therefore, means internalising the system of knowledge, cultural representations and values of the society, the epoch, the social birth group and especially the group in which the child grows up. Not only do words carry meaning, but because of this they also carry 'values' and 'emotions'. Learning to talk also means learning to think and to live. But this is not to say that later, when the child has grown up, it will not think and live differently.

Let us continue this analysis of language acquisition, which begins when a child is around the age of nine to ten months and

---

8 de Boysson-Bardies, *Comment la parole vient aux enfants*, 149.

continues until it is eighteen to twenty months, and note – this is fundamental – that it is at this point that the child develops simultaneously an awareness of self and the ability to represent the world (to itself) and to multiply its symbolic practices. This occurs as the social, affective and cognitive exchanges between adults and child increase in number. These reciprocal exchanges provide the child with the model of its language and at the same time with models of psychological and social behaviour. Even before learning to walk, but especially once it does, the child discovers the characteristics of solid objects (whether stationary or moving), of liquids, of space, in short of the surrounding physical world. The child is thus capable of making 'deductions' about the nature of its physical and social world even before it possesses the appropriate words to express them.

To conclude, we can now step back and take a global view of the nature and role of language in the functioning of societies and in the construction of the subject. Language occupies two sites at once: on the one hand, the field of intersubjective relations, therefore making it crucial to the life of societies; and on the other hand, it is immanent to the consciousness of each speaker of a particular language, where it functions as the inner speech that each person addresses to him- or herself. This inner speech is none other than the language of the linguistic community to which the subject belongs. In the field of intersubjective relations, to understand what others are telling us is to experience immediately that others are thereby manifesting an intentional life, which makes them alter egos.[9] Yet as a subject, I can never gain direct access to the meaning actually intended by others. I can do this only through the mediation of words and gestures, and therefore through the mediation of the signifiers the other uses in order to address me. The same is true for the other's relation to me. In the last analysis, then, I do not have access to the consciousness and the mind of others as they experience them. The other can lie to me, just as I can lie to them. They can think and pursue something other than what

9   M. Caveing, *Le problème des objets dans la pensée mathématique* (Paris: Vrin, 2004), 152–153.

they tell me, and so on. We all know that words (and more generally symbols) can have several meanings, and that to truly understand them we must know how to interpret them, to submit them to a hermeneutic analysis. In this way, language has a double function in societies: as communication, on the one hand; and, on the other, as an instrument for experiencing the other as a subject, a non-ego, which is also an ego but one with which we can be neither fused nor confused, a 'transcendent' subject. While it connects people, language also separates them.

In addition, and to the same extent, language unites the subject with himself at the same time as it allows the subject to step back and reflect on himself, on others, on the surrounding world, to analyse and to decide. This is the work of inner speech. Consciousness is inhabited by language, by a language of which it is not the origin and which continually accompanies the states and acts of the subject in the form of inner speech, without the subject having willed it.[10] Inner speech is governed by the linguistic system of this language and is therefore governed by structural constraints that the subject must unconsciously or consciously respect in order to make himself understood to himself and others. But this language is also structured by the flow of time, as is consciousness, since both exist only in and by the succession of past, present and future. With the crucial particularity that consciousness can at any moment be both present to and absent from the moment experienced. And this is because at any moment, the mind can imagine past facts and make them present to consciousness, or transport the subject to a future that does not yet exist. That is the power and the role of the imagination.

The power of the imagination is also found in a crucial feature of everyday language, and that is its metaphoric character. Let me give a few examples: 'to keep a stiff upper lip'; it is also said of someone that he is 'out to lunch'. You can hear such expressions as 'What you just said goes straight to my heart'; or 'Your explanation doesn't hold water'; 'Lay it on the table'; 'Let him stew a while'; 'We're at a

---

10   Ibid., 140.

cross-roads'; 'Let's dig into the matter'; 'hit the spot'. English speakers intuitively understand the meaning of each of these metaphors, and new ones come online every day. So just what is a metaphor? It is a form of thought and language that is doubly symbolic, in the sense that the words used – 'upper lip', 'heart', 'to stew' – have another meaning once they are rerouted from their original sense. A metaphor uses images to express ideas that could perhaps be expressed in more abstract terms, although often this is not possible. According to Lakoff and Johnson's definition: 'The essence of metaphor is understanding and experiencing one kind of thing *in terms of another*.'[11]

We thus understand from words and images that have been diverted from their literal meaning – 'to stew', 'out to lunch' – something other than what they signify. Thus, linguistic metaphors indeed function as symbols. The words and images used refer to concrete experiences ('meat stews', for example), on which the mind hangs its metaphors and in terms of which we understand them. Metaphors convey a figurative understanding of realities or complex situations that would need a lengthy development if described using abstract concepts. They therefore have explanatory power; we can use the term 'metaphorical concepts' in talking about them, keeping in mind that the explanatory part of a metaphor goes no further than what the image of the phenomenon it uses as raw material can suggest to the mind (the fact of stewing). That is why a metaphor often provides only a partial comprehension of what it describes, whether it be our inner feelings, our aesthetic experiences, our moral practices, and so on. Let me add that metaphors are not the only means the mind has to move from the literal to the figurative. If metaphor is first of all a means of thinking one thing in terms of another, we can also use one entity in place of another, for example, instead of saying 'Get yourself over here,' we can say more crudely, 'Get your butt over here,' the part being taken for the whole. In this case, the mind calls not on metaphors, but on metonymies, for instance: 'I bought a two-wheeler.'

---

11   G. Lakoff and M. Johnson, *Metaphors We Live By* (Chicago: University of Chicago Press, 1980), 5; my emphasis.

Religious systems make great use of metonymies, like the symbolic metonymy of the dove to designate the Holy Spirit in Christianity. I will return to religious symbolisms at the end of this book.

In conclusion, metaphor and metonymy are not merely linguistic phenomena. They are phenomena that have to do in the first place with thought and action; they are a sort of 'imaginative rationality',[12] as Lakoff so elegantly puts it, a rationality combining ideas and images that functions in everyday life and draws on our daily experiences. It must be stressed that this imaginative reasoning proceeds basically by drawing *analogies* between two or several facts, actions or situations, or between living and nonliving beings: 'He is as stubborn as a mule'; 'You can't budge him, he's rock solid.' The logic of imaginative reasoning is a logic of analogy, and this logic is not restricted to daily life. It is the bedrock of poetry, on the one hand, and of mythic thought, on the other. Verlaine's 'les sanglots longs des violons de l'automne bercent mon coeur d'une langueur monotone' again comes to mind,[13] as does the mythological figure of the Amerindian Coyote, who is a demiurge, master of salmon and womaniser with a snakelike penis. Once again, with these analogies imagined by the mind, we find ourselves surrounded by symbols. We can therefore no longer postpone an examination of the symbolic function.

---

12   Ibid., 193.

13   The music of words opens our minds to music itself, which affects us by more than its sounds and rhythms, and can conjure up the four seasons of the year, as in the case of Vivaldi.

CHAPTER FOUR

The Symbolic Function

To symbolise is to produce signs that have meaning. A sign that has meaning is a signifier, whatever its nature. The universe of the symbolic is thus the set of all past and present signifiers and all possible signifieds. The symbolic function is what enables us to associate in a stable fashion one psychic state with another. That is how English speakers repeatedly associate the word 'cow' with the animal the word designates. The symbolic function is pre-inscribed – that is to say genetically inscribed – in our psyche and in our entire body. It is involved in all forms of thought and action humankind has invented until now and will be in all those we invent in the future.

All signifiers are signs that refer to something other than themselves, whereby this thing takes on meaning for everyone who produces or receives these signs. In 1910, Ferdinand de Saussure had envisaged a discipline, semiology, that would study and explain 'the social life of signs', and which would thus reach beyond linguistics; this was a limitless project that got no further than its ambitious beginnings. The difficulty lay in the fact that nearly everything can be or become the sign of something, which makes a general, global classification of signs nearly impossible. C. S. Peirce tackled the problem without ever resolving it.[1] He analysed signs from three standpoints: the sign itself (sound, gesture, mental representation, spoken word, written form, etc.); the sign as it relates to its 'object'; and the sign as it relates to its interpreter. We shall restrict ourselves to commenting on the three categories into which Peirce divided signs according to their relation with their object: signs as indications, or 'indices'; signs as 'icons'; and signs as 'symbols'. But let us

---

1   C. S. Peirce, *Writings on Semiotics* (Chapel Hill: University of North Carolina Press, 1991).

not forget that all these signs have meaning and that all are therefore 'symbols'.

An index is a sign that has a physical connection with the object it indicates. It is the paw print of a bear in the snow, in which a tracker will read the animal's size, its sex, the time elapsed since its passage and the direction in which it is moving. The mental image of the bear will immediately spring to mind, call up, through inner speech, the word for the animal and unconsciously reactivate all of the cultural representations and emotions connected with the bear in his society and in his personal experience. It is a trace of blood a killer leaves at the scene of his crime, which will allow the police to identify his DNA. It is the involuntary signs of weakness, good health or despair, produced by the body of those who are sick, desperate or joyful, but which the doctor, friend, et cetera observes and interprets.[2] Smoke rising from a chimney means that someone has made a fire. A bear's paw print, blood, and smoke are all signs in the present that refer to past events; they are all 'indices'. But for a driver, the red light at an intersection means stop, do not go through; the green light means it is possible to go. A finger on the lips is a discreet signal to another to keep quiet. Here the sign concerns the future.

Peirce termed 'icons' all signs that possess a certain formal resemblance to the object they refer to, such as van Gogh's self-portrait, or the giant portraits of Mao Zedong or Stalin. Another kind of icon is a road sign bearing the silhouette of a wild boar or a deer at the entrance to a forest, which tells drivers of the risk of suddenly coming upon one or several of these animals. Another type of icon is that which adorns Orthodox churches, representing the Virgin Mary and the Child Jesus, or the archangel Gabriel announcing to Mary that she

---

2   We cannot leave out Aristotle and the semiotic theory he developed in his *Prior Analytics*, where he takes as an example the fact that if a woman has milk, it is the sign she has borne a child, but the converse is not true. See Aristotle, *Organon*, vol. 3, *Prior Analytics*. Aristotle analyses the signs that necessarily or probably demonstrate the existence or production of something else. See also G. G. Granger, *La Théorie aristotélicienne de la science* (Paris: Aubier, 1976).

would bear a son who would be the Messiah long awaited by the Jewish people. Yet another icon is the mental image of the bear I have in my head.

The relationship of similitude between a silhouette of a deer and the animal on a road sign is easy to understand. On the other hand, for a non-Christian, the relationship is much less easy to perceive in the case of religious icons, whether Greek, Russian or Bulgarian. The portraits of Mary and Jesus are purely imaginary. They are idealised representations of figures who no doubt existed, but whose features no one has passed on to us. And the icon painter escalated the imaginary when he painted the archangel Gabriel (who we may believe to have never existed) in human likeness with wings on his back (a sign that he is 'truly' an angel). It is therefore hard for the non-Christian to understand the theological meaning of this picture, even if, independently, he can appreciate its beauty and admire it.

Let us move on to the signs Peirce classified as 'symbols', those for which there is no relationship of similitude between the sign and the thing signified, but an arbitrary relation determined by convention. Such are the words of a spoken language, and the same words if they are written, whatever the system used: alphabetic, ideographic, pictographic, et cetera. To these must be added the gestural systems that make up the different languages invented to communicate with the deaf and so that the deaf may communicate with each other. And then there is the drummed language of the Yangere people of Zaire, whose drumbeats send messages deep into the forest, for instance to tell a hunter to hurry back because his wife has just given birth. Nor should we forget Morse code and the various languages invented by sailors or soldiers to communicate their messages.

I could go on and on with examples of symbols. The blue, white and red French flag, the red flag of the communist parties bearing the hammer and sickle, symbols of the (hoped for) alliance between peasants and workers, or the black flag of the anarchists. These symbols refer to the existence of social groups that have chosen them as emblems of their identity, their values; though everyone knows that communists and anarchists hold opposite views on the role of the state and the nature of the society they would like to establish.

To conclude, I have chosen a strong symbol – '*Je suis Charlie*' – which emerged in France following the assassination on 7 January 2015 by two terrorists, claiming to be from the Yemenite branch of al-Qaida, of twelve artists and editors from the satirical magazine *Charlie Hebdo*, together with two policemen. The symbol appeared in the streets, brandished by hundreds of thousands of people gathered to show their indignation, their anger and their solidarity with the victims, and above all their will and desire to defend a 'sacred' principle of the French Republic: freedom of speech.

They came, even if some demonstrators did not share the magazine's irreverent tone, qualified by religious believers as blasphemous. In brandishing '*Je suis Charlie*', they were identifying with the victims and defending a right that entailed the possibility for a journal like *Charlie Hebdo* to exist but which went far beyond the issue of its existence. We have the birth certificate of this symbol. It was invented on the spot by Joachim Roncin, the artistic director of a small free magazine, *Stylist*, who, shocked by the massacre, had written on his computer screen: '*Je suis Charlie*'.[3] For a moment, Roncin worried that these words might offend the friends of *Charlie*. But colleagues reassured him, and a journalist tweeted the three words, which were immediately taken up and reproduced by tens of thousands of people. The success was tremendous. The symbol leaped borders and found itself carried in the streets or posted on the walls of Berlin, London, New York, Madrid and many other capitals by demonstrators who chose this means to attest that they shared the same values as the French who had taken to the streets in Paris. But following the assassination – after the *Charlie Hebdo* massacre – of four Jewish persons by

---

3   *Libération*, 14 January 2015, 14

Amedy Coulibaly, who claimed affiliation with Daesh, France also saw a counter-symbol, *'Je suis Coulibaly'*, diffused in social media networks by anonymous followers who adopted it to show their approval of these crimes and their agreement with the justifications advanced by their authors.

Among the varieties of symbols, mathematical symbols call for a separate treatment;[4] these are numbers, geometrical figures, algebraic formulae and so on. They are of a completely different nature from those of the symbols discussed above: flags, emblems, slogans, writing systems and so on. Among the mathematical symbols, we must distinguish those that present a likeness, such as the isosceles triangle drawn on the board and analysed for the students by their math teacher, and the 'linguistic' symbols, such as a and b in the formula $(a + b)2 = a2 + b2 + 2ab$, or the Greek letter Π (pi), symbol for the number that represents the constant relation between the circumference of a circle and its diameter. If the drawing on the board may represent something for those who have no mathematical knowledge, the signs $\sqrt{}$, Π or the formula $y = f(x)$ mean nothing to them. To understand these symbols, the person would have to become a mathematician and perform the conceptual operations that give them meaning. Failing that, all these symbols will remain a mystery, dead signs.

Let us come back to the example of the drawing of an isosceles triangle. The drawing is a physical representation of a mathematical 'object' that belongs to the field of Euclidian geometry and is defined by its axioms. Yet the word 'object', as Maurice Caveing showed, is inappropriate, for it carries various ontological representations and reifications.[5] Mathematical objects are ideal 'beings', idealities that exist only in mathematical theories. Isosceles triangles are not found

---

4   Cf. M. Serfati, *La Révolution symbolique. La constitution de l'écriture symbolique mathématique* (Paris: Pétra, 2005).

5   Caveing, *Le problème des objets dans la pensée mathématique*, 21. I take this opportunity to say that my debt to the work of Maurice Caveing is immense and goes well beyond mathematics and philosophy.

in nature, much less 'transfinite' numbers; the mathematical ideality known as 'triangle', therefore, cannot come from an act of perception but is the result of an operation of construction governed by rules. The triangle drawn is therefore one of the forms – they are infinite in number – that corresponds to the essential properties of the triangle as a 'theoretical ideality'. The triangle cannot be drawn. The triangle, as a mathematical ideality, is unique. Its graphic representations, from the standpoint of shape (degrees of the angles) as well as size (length of the sides), are infinite.

What does the theoretical activity of a mathematician consist of, then? It means solving problems and proving theorems.[6] Its objects are relations and systems of relations. By applying various types of conceptual operations to these relations, the mathematician builds mathematical objects, in other words, idealities, which are clusters of relations that themselves open onto other relations. Mathematical thinking thus works by 'successive mediations that form a chain by connecting relations with each other'.[7] The resulting relations, operations and idealities are expressed in a technical language belonging to the field of mathematics, a formal language made up of symbols that have no meaning for nonmathematicians. The plus (+) and minus (-) signs are symbols for the operations of addition and subtraction; the radical ($\sqrt{}$) is the symbol for the extraction of a root, which can be square ($2\sqrt{}$) or cube ($3\sqrt{}$), et cetera. Mathematical idealities, therefore, exist purely in and through this operational activity that supposes the mediation of its own language, which is universal. Certain symbols in the language of mathematics are borrowed from spoken languages, such as the words 'group', 'ring', 'body', 'root', 'matrix', 'lattice', or verbs like 'extract' and 'extend'. But the nonlinguistic words and symbols are basically unequivocal, and their meaning depends strictly on the operations they express. Nothing in these symbols leaves room for the mathematician's subjectivity; there is

---

6   Ibid., 28.
7   Ibid., 262.

nothing equivocal about them that might invite the possibility of wordplay or a hermeneutic.

Each time a mathematician performs a sequence of operations and reactivates their meanings, they are no longer, as the standardised subject of these operations, the empirical self of everyday life. For the only way they can operate is by placing themselves within a domain of idealities constituted as a domain of preestablished truths, and the only way they can carry out this task is by submitting to the content of proven theorems. This is true for all mathematicians, French, Russian or Chinese. Once obtained, the results of mathematicians' work, which is to produce and demonstrate truths that each can in turn repeat and verify, become both transcultural and transtemporal. They are now detached from the time, the society and the mathematician who first produced the demonstration, whether it was Euclid, Descartes, Hilbert or Cantor. The world of mathematics is thus one where each subject finds him- or herself in a relation of transparent reciprocal exchange with all other mathematicians, repeating the same operations and obtaining the same results. These form, for mathematicians, a field of idealities and norms that envelop them and which they expand by their discoveries, but which always transcends them and remains open to other systems of relations. Mathematicians' acts make them, as producers of universal knowledge, universal subjects.

Furthermore, the development of mathematics since the end of the nineteenth century has increasingly freed it from all reference to the empirical intuition that was originally connected with Euclidian geometry and with the physics that had been associated with it. But even in Euclidian geometry, there was, as Descartes pointed out, the distinction between the figure of a triangle and its concept. And non-Euclidian geometries have completely eliminated the intuition of the three-dimensional space in which we move.[8] Geometry has

---

8   The case of non-Euclidian geometries is far from the only example of elimination of empirical intuition in mathematics.

thus moved towards increasing abstraction and formalism, without it ever being possible to call into doubt either the reality of its new objects or the truth of their demonstrations. Paradoxically – given its ideal character – mathematics is still the area of knowledge that attests to the capacity of the human mind to produce objective knowledge that transcends time and cultural worlds. Descartes knew this – even if he postulated that mathematical truth was, in the final analysis, grounded in God (the Christian God) when he wrote: 'For if it happened that an individual, even when asleep, had some very distinct idea, as, for example, if a geometer should discover some new demonstration, the circumstance of his being asleep would not militate against its truth.'[9]

To conclude this all-too-rapid analysis of the symbolic function, allow me to underscore five important features.

1. Any sign always either stands for something else, or is a function of something else (Hjelmslev).[10]

2. A sign always obeys a code and is a coded access to a referent. A sign therefore transmits information to those who know the code.

3. A sign as signifier can refer to one or several signifieds at the same time.

4. Signs and the necessary access codes can never contain more information or other types of information than that invested in them by their original inventers and by all those who in turn put them to new uses.

5. The symbolic function exceeds the mind and the body. It pervades everything people do, everything people invest with meaning:

---

9 R. Descartes, *Discourse on the Method of Rightly Conducting the Reason and Seeking the Truth in the Sciences*, ed. C. W. Eliot (New York: P. F. Collier & Son, 1909). M. Caveing also cites Plato, who, in his *Theaetetus*, has Socrates say: 'Now call to mind whether . . . you have never ventured, even in sleep, to say to yourself that the odd is, after all, certainly even, or anything of that sort' (190).

10 L. Hjelmslev, *Prolégomènes à une théorie du langage* (Paris: Minuit, 1968 [1943], chap. 13).

churches, temples, statues, mountains, the sun, the moon, et cetera.

All signs, whatever they may be – including mathematical symbols[11] – were imagined before being used.

---

11   It should be remembered that mathematical symbols symbolise the operations and objects in the different 'calculations' carried out by mathematicians: elementary arithmetical calculations, algebraic calculations, functional calculus, vector calculus, matrical calculus, tensor calculus, etc.

CHAPTER FIVE

What Is Imagining?

Let us take a few examples of imagining from different contexts.

Ego (man or woman) to him- or herself – inner speech:
- I will always see my mother's face when she learned of my father's accident.
- I would never have imagined that of him.
- All these killings; the Mafia is probably behind them.
- I can already see where I'm going to put the table.

Ego (man or woman) to Alter (man or woman) – familiar context, a relative, friend, neighbour:
- Imagine my ex-husband's face when he saw me with Jacques.
- Who does he think he is? Maybe he imagines we've forgotten where he comes from?
- Ten years ago I'd never have imagined that, with all their diplomas, my children would be unemployed.
- You can't imagine he's going to get away with it.

Ego (man or woman) in a professional context:
- A philosopher: Imagine a world without God (gods).
- A priest: The tomb was empty; Jesus had risen.
- A general: Let's imagine the enemy is attacking from this side.
- A mathematician: Let us now suppose that two parallel lines in the same plane meet at infinity; that would contradict one of Euclid's postulates.

- A politician: When they attacked Iraq and overthrew Saddam Hussein's regime, the Americans certainly didn't imagine what would happen next.
- An economist: Great Britain adopting the Euro is unimaginable.
- A poet (Raymond Queneau): 'If you imagine my girl, my dear, that [love] is going to last, last, last forever.'

To extend this analysis of the forms and effects of the capacity to imagine and to imagine oneself, we need to come back to the analysis of the relationship between the mind and consciousness. We have seen that consciousness of the present is always broader than the present moment, since the immediate past remains attached and present consciousness is already involved in an immediate future. But the capacity to imagine goes beyond these different bits of time clinging to the present. It explores all of the possibilities offered by inner consciousness of time. It allows a human being, at every moment, to be both present and not present.

I am there, in my study; I am looking at an orchid that has come into bloom and, at the same time, I 'see' before me once again the greenhouse where my mother used to grow her flowers. When I 'look at' the orchid, I am not imagining it; I perceive it, I see it 'in person'. But at the same time, I see more of it than I actually perceive because even though the flower presents only one of its sides, when I 'see' it, knowing that it has more than one side, I represent it to myself, implicitly bearing in mind all the sides I do not perceive. Furthermore, as I look at the orchid, my mind transports me to the greenhouse, now gone, of my mother, who is now gone as well. At the very moment when the orchid manifested itself directly to my consciousness, the image and memory of the greenhouse also filled my conscious mind, and therefore the plant began, for a moment, to exist not as the orchid I was looking at, but as a presence-absence, a presence that made an absence present to me. I thus found myself looking at a flower and imagining a greenhouse that had once existed in my life but no longer exists.

We have just encountered one form of the imagination: that which allows me to remember, to bring back 'to life' a past that once existed but no longer does. This indicates a way to continue the inventory of the forms of the imagination. The forms are different and differ according to the nature of the objects, of the imagined realities and according to the time in which the mind places them, situates them, in the past, the present or the future. Applying these criteria, we can distinguish at least eight forms of imaginary activities, which are available at all times to a thinking subject.

The reality imagined either

1. really existed, but no longer does;

   I can still see my mother's face.

2. really exists, but somewhere else;

   I see exactly where they live.

3. will surely exist in the future;

   Next year I will be retired, and I hope to enjoy it.

4. will perhaps exist in the future;

   One day I would like to visit South India.

5. did not exist in the past;

   Until the twentieth century, no man had flown in the sky.

6. may have existed in the past;

   I imagine that the emperor of China may have heard that the Roman Empire existed.

7. cannot now or ever exist; or

   No man will ever be able to jump to a height of forty metres.

8. is impossible, but nevertheless possible.

   The tomb was empty; Jesus had risen.

Putting together the examples contained in the above table of the possible relationships between the mind of someone who imagines, and the 'things' he or she imagines, we get an approximate representation (to be completed) of what is covered by the notion of 'imagined'.

It is immediately clear that everything that is imagined is not imaginary, and that we can therefore isolate the reasons that determine whether what is imagined is or is not imaginary. Let us take another look at the eight cases listed above. We see that:

- Cases 1 and 2 refer to something imagined that is not imaginary. Both refer to realities that were possible at one point and then came into existence and became real.
- Case 3 refers to an imagined but not imaginary possibility that will certainly become a reality (retirement in six months) if the person does not die before then.
- Case 4 refers to an imagined possibility (a trip to South India) that may never be realised. In this event, in time the imagined would become imaginary.
- Case 5 refers to realities that were long imaginary (flying in the sky) and later became feasible. The imaginary has given way to the non-imaginary imagined, to a possibility now realisable and realised.
- Case 6 refers to an imaginable possibility that may or may not be purely imaginary.
- Case 7 refers to objectively unrealisable possibilities, and therefore to purely imaginary imagineds.
- Case 8 refers to the vast domain of religions, myths, rites and magic, that is, to imaginable realities whose existence is counter-intuitive and opposed to our knowledge of the possible of every-day experience. Yet these realities are considered to be possible, though not in terms of the reality with which humankind usually deals. This is the domain of the impossible, the unbelievable that is nevertheless posited as possible and believable. Here, the imaginary appears *more* real than everything we can imagine because it has become the portal to surreality that is the very basis of the real that humankind faces daily.[1]

---

1   Conversely, the Shoah existed, but it is difficult to imagine what it was for the millions of men, women and children who were its victims.

We can add a ninth case to this list: that of real facts that defeat the imagination, such as the example of someone hostile to 'American imperialism', who refuses to believe that Armstrong really walked on the moon, and for whom the whole story is a lie propagated by the Americans by means of photos faked in a studio.

We see, then, that the power of the imagination is to enable our mind and our actions to confront a network of opposing aspects of our experience of our world and ourselves; namely, such oppositions as those between

representable	unrepresentable
possible	impossible
certain	uncertain
probable	improbable
predictable	unpredictable
believable	unbelievable

These opposites also combine with each other. The possible can be certain or probable, predictable or unpredictable, and so on. Thus, the cursor between the non-imaginary imagined and the imaginary imagined moves through these combinations, some of which draw no clear line between the non-imaginary and the imaginary: for example, imagining facts that historians suppose may have existed in the period under analysis, but for which they do not yet have irrefutable proof. There remain imagined phenomena that may or may not be imaginary. But this is not the case for the miracles and wonders attributed to men and the gods in myths and religions. For believers, these are real, not imaginary.

The question is: What leap must the mind make in order to believe the unbelievable? In order to do this, clearly, the mind must stop applying the everyday criteria it uses to distinguish between possible and impossible, to define what is real. To be sure. But why make such a leap in the first place? What are the reasons, the forces that drive a person to believe and to want others to believe what this person believes? For to believe means to overcome one's doubts, set them aside in order to emerge into the light of the self-evident truths of one's faith (faith in Mao Zedong, faith in Muhammad and in the Koran, faith in the ancestors, and so on). In this case, symbols take on a different meaning. It is no longer humans who, with the help of symbols they have invented, signify to themselves something that first existed only through their thought processes and in their minds. Symbols become the signs of the revelations the ancestors – Moses, the future Buddha, Muhammad, and so on – received from the gods, or from God; and these revelations oblige those who have received them to change the way they live. But a revelation can also come to a philosopher like Heidegger, who, probing the roots of a few words in Ancient Greek and German (languages proclaimed to be 'the languages of philosophy' par excellence), begins listening to the Being of the Being beyond the being of the beings (*sic*).

With these examples in mind, we can measure the power of the imagination.

1. It enables us to represent to ourselves realities that no longer exist, or that do not exist, or that exist elsewhere, or that will perhaps or never exist, that should not exist but nevertheless do, et cetera.

2. It enables us to represent to ourselves facts, situations and persons whose existence we have never attested but which others report to us (relatives, neighbours, journalists, history professors, etc.). And we do the same with regard to others when we tell someone about something he or she has not witnessed. But then the question arises: How much credit should we lend to these accounts; what truth value do they have?

3. This question leads us to look at 'what is behind' the facts, words and acts, and to suspect that, behind appearances, behind what is visible and known, there is something more that could be the unknown reason and explanation for what is apparent, visible and known.

4. It enables us, when circumstances require or the context allows, to think and/or do otherwise, to look for other ways of demonstrating a theorem, alternatives to attain a goal, et cetera. For

example, if, as the mathematician Desargues did in 1639, we consider 'parallels going in the same direction and meeting in infinity as having the same status as any point in the plane',[2] we violate a basic rule of Euclidian geometry that says that parallel lines are lines in a same plane that never meet no matter how far they are extended.[3] In cancelling this rule, Desargues opened the way for a new field of mathematics, albeit one which he did not develop himself.

By operating in these four fields of possibility, imagination is therefore one of the preconditions of all forms of thought and action deployed by humankind – art forms, religions, scientific knowledge, military strategies, kinship relations, material techniques, forms of power and their ideological legitimisations, and so on. All these forms of thought and action have different contents and engender specific structures depending on whether they rely mainly on one or the other of the two logics organising our thoughts and actions. In one logic, the possible and the impossible are mutually exclusive; in the other, they are not.

Scientific knowledge, material techniques and their like are governed by the first logic. Religions, myths, tales and so forth are governed by the second. Between these two poles lie all fields of existence and experience. To illustrate this opposition, I will say that at one pole, we would find mathematics and various systems of logic; and at the other, forms of mystical thought, for example, in the West the experience of fusion with God (as described by Teresa of Ávila), or in India fusion with a personally chosen god to whom a person offers daily acts of devotion (*bhakti*) in the hope of liberation after death from the cycle of rebirths (*samsara*). There are thus several forms of imaginary, whose status varies with whether people believe, do not or no longer believe, or more or less believe. The many forms of imaginary that exist (or will come to exist) operate between these two poles:

---

2 Caveing, *Le problème des objets dans la pensée mathématique*, 61.
3 Ibid.

on the one hand, the imaginary recognised and experienced as such (in play, for instance); and on the other hand, the imaginary that has been transmuted, transfigured into surreality (in religions, for example).

As we did for language acquisition, let us look at how a child experiences these different and opposing types of imaginary. To do this we will call on the innovative studies of the American psychologist Paul Harris and his team on the work of the imagination, and more particularly on its development and uses in the child.[4] When we leave the world of children's games for those of adults, we will turn to Roberte Hamayon's remarkable book *Jouer. Une étude anthropologique* (*Why We Play: An anthropological study*).[5]

Let me recall the guiding principle of our analyses: everything, whether it is imaginary or not, has first of all been imagined. Everything that is imagined can be signified. Everything that is signified is signified using *specific* signifiers: sounds, words, sculptures, rites, games and so on. So what is going to differentiate for the child what belongs to the domain of the non-imaginary imagined and what belongs to the imaginary imagined? The criteria are: the nature of what is imagined by the mind; and the nature of the signifier chosen to signify it.

The results of combining these two components are going, depending on the nature of each, to engender objects endowed with different forms and degrees of reality: from purely mental reality to mental reality materialised, from virtual reality to the virtual that has become real, from the ideal to the unreal, from the unreal to the surreal.

Here are two simple examples:

1. Something imagined that is not imaginary
    a) signified: the real map of a city, as an image of the city, published by the city's tourism office and distributed free of charge to visitors who ask for it

---

4   P. Harris, *The Work of the Imagination* (Hoboken, NJ: Blackwell Publishers, 2000).

5   R. Hamayon, *Jouer. Une étude anthropologique* (Paris: La Découverte, 2012).

      b) signifier: the material drawing of the streets and avenues with their names and orientation, and the locations of monuments to visit, all printed on a piece of paper in black and white or in colour

2. Something imagined that is purely imaginary
      a) signified: the adventures of *Tintin and the Temple of the Sun*
      b) signifier: the drawings and the words of Hergé's story printed on paper and made into a book

Depending on what they have to signify, the drawings, words and materials on which they are printed do not have the same meaning or the same social standing (practical object: town map; fun object: a Tintin book). The city map is not an imaginary object, because it refers to a reality, the city, which exists independently of the map and outside the mind of the tourist who wants to visit it. Tintin's world does not exist anywhere except in the mind of Hergé, his inventor, and in the minds of readers who in turn make this unreal world exist for the time it takes to read the book, provided they understand the drawings and the story. Tintin's world exists, then, but as an ideal presence in people's minds; it has no real reference point in the outside world (except for T-shirts, figurines, posters, books and films, all of which are industrially manufactured imitations that are lucrative commercial objects in the real world). With the Tintin book and its commercial offshoots, we not only have one foot in the art world, but also one in the world of fairy tales, legends, myths, science fiction movies: *Terminator, Star Wars*, and so on.

    Having made these conceptual distinctions, we will now go on to analyse the nature and role of the imagination in three domains, successively: play, the arts and religions.

CHAPTER SIX

What Is Play?

Play is a universal activity that is common to humans, and to many animals.[1] Who has not smiled in amusement at two puppies playing, as they pounce on each other and bite without actually biting? Because actually biting is no longer playing; it is fighting. Playing means *playing at*, pretending to fight. Playing is 'pretending', it is 'make believe'.[2] All humans played in childhood, but it is only gradually that children begin to play. Observation tells us that it is towards the end of the second year, at more or less the same time as they begin to speak the language spoken to them, that their imagination has developed and that they begin to play, on their own or with others. Playing alone with their stuffed bear or doll, later playing papa and mama, doctor and patient, with others. And then comes the succession of games of 'let's pretend' and 'role play'. Once the capacity to play has appeared, it does not disappear with childhood. It persists for the rest of life.[3]

For a two-year-old, playing alone means inventing an imaginary world where there are no set rules, but simply the succession of acts by which the child pretends to do something.[4] She scolds her teddy bear because it has wet on the floor, pretending to wipe up the inexistent puddle. The child is playing and knows she is playing. The child attributes intentions and actions to her stuffed bear in the knowledge that her bear did not and cannot do anything. To construct the imaginary world they invent when playing, children imitate, simulate real acts and situations they have experienced or observed in the real

---

1 J. Huizinga, *Homo Ludens: A Study of the Play-Element in Culture* (London and New York: Routledge & Kegan Paul, 1949 [1938]).

2 Let us recall the importance of Jean Piaget and his groundbreaking book *The Construction of Reality in the Child* (London and New York: Routledge & Kegan Paul, 1999 [1927]).

3 Harris, *The Work of the Imagination*, 27.

4 D. W. Winnicott, *Playing and Reality* (London and New York: Routledge, 1989 [1971]).

world and whose meaning they have understood. Children understand the relationship between a cause and its consequences (weeing
on the floor makes a mess), the sequence of acts they must perform to
wipe up the (imaginary) urine, et cetera. So they know what one does
when not playing, and at the same time that they are not 'really' doing
what they imitate virtually. In role play, children give themselves a
role and an identity. If there are several players, they allocate the
different (and often opposing) but complementary roles, such as
those of cowboys and Indians. We thus observe that they use words
and gestures that correspond to their role and even simulate the
emotions their character would feel if they were really wounded or
captured.[5] Yet the actions, gestures, and so forth that children imitate
both resemble and differ from those gestures and acts imitated.[6] For
to imitate is at once to reproduce and to reinvent.

In short, for children, playing means involving themselves physically, mentally and emotionally in the imaginary world they create in
play. And they are often so caught up in their game that they must be
torn away at bedtime. Adults do the same thing when they are so
absorbed in a novel or a movie that they forget to eat.[7] When reading
a gripping novel, a person often identifies with the main protagonist
and 'is' that person, suffering with them while living their (imaginary)
life. From play we have already moved on to the world of art, which
we will analyse in the next chapter.

Coming back to role play and the various degrees of identification it entails with the character being played, it is doubtless in the
so-called 'Second Life' computer game that the imagined and imaginary identification is the most extreme, even endangering the player's
mental stability.[8] In these games, players identify with one or several

---

5   Harris, *The Work of the Imagination*, 30–31.

6   G. Bateson: 'What is characteristic of "play" is that this is a name for contexts in
which the constituent acts have a different sort of relevance and organization from that
which they would have had in non-play.' *Mind and Nature: A Necessary Unity* (New York:
Dutton, 1979), 125.

7   Harris, *The Work of the Imagination*, 48–54. 'Absorption in a pretence: Continuities
between children and adults.'

8   Hamayon, *Jouer*, 139.

'avatars', which they choose and through which they begin to 'live' one or several virtual lives. Some players identify so strongly with their avatar – an 'unreal' man or woman – and become so emotionally involved in the adventures of their double that they no longer know who they 'really' are. Apart from eating and drinking, and sleeping a little, their life is one with that of their double. Their being merges with the unreal being which they themselves have created, and which does not exist outside this imagined and imaginary world. The danger they run is a simple one: ultimately it is the loss of all concrete existential reference points and the inner dissolution of the 'lost' self. A person 'becomes lost' when they (mis)take a virtual world for a real world, with the ultimate risk of going 'mad'.

Nevertheless, it is also possible to play 'for the fun of it'. Psychologists tell us that when young children play 'pretend', they are at the same time exploring the real world that they have left by playing. Alternatively, when a game entails winning or losing, a person can also join the game with a single desire: to win. In fact, that is the primary motive in gambling, for in that case, winning means winning money and losing means losing money. And the outcome of the game has positive or negative effects on real life, on the players' 'outside lives' (those who bet on the horses, for example).[9]

We can also analyse games from another angle, considering the role of chance, as opposed to the player's ability, in determining the outcome. In certain games, chance is master (roulette, dice). For others (card games), chance comes in when the cards are dealt and the players begin to play their hand. For others still (chess), the setup is the same for both players; the outcome will be determined by the players' strategies and degree of practice. Finally, for still others, the games played by amateurs-turned-professionals (basketball, football, rugby, skiing, etc.), the players must acquire (ideomotor) experience of the concrete on-the-ground situations, which are constantly

---

9 This category of play is in contradiction with Benvéniste's definition of play as 'an activity with rules whose purpose is itself and does not aim to alter reality in a useful way'. *Deucalion* (1947), cited in Hamayon, 80.

changing; for this they must undergo regular training. Playing as an amateur and playing as a professional are two opposing ways of playing which nevertheless share several features. In both cases, the confrontation between the two teams is not a real battle, even if at the end there is a winner and a loser, or the game ends in a tie, with neither loser nor winner. In both cases, the players play on opposing teams, which implies that each player cooperates with the others on his team and fights against those of the other team, surpassing them through their performance. In both cases, players and spectators have left their everyday world and find themselves in another world, which will last for the duration of the game. The match is a spectacle put on for the public by the players who, in turn, win or lose reputation and fame in the process. The spectacle arouses emotions and passions in each team's supporters, who sometimes pour down onto the playing field to threaten the referee and the players of the 'other' team for having inflicted a defeat with which they do not agree.[10] The spectators have paid to watch and to dream; the players are paid to make them dream; and behind the players and spectators are the clubs, which lose or win money. In the end, everyone comes back to earth and the 'real' world.

What constant lies at the heart of the multiple forms of games that exist, despite the diversity of their purposes? In order to play, it is always necessary to invent a context distinct from that of everyday life. To play is to subscribe to a fictional framework involving chance, which takes on a real existence during play.[11] Games are an imagined world in which the player measures his or her experience with chance. When it is achieved, this world remains, and can only remain, 'unreal' compared with the reality of life in society that precedes the game and reappears afterwards; for even if, in order to play, we interrupt the flow of constraints and obligations with which we all must contend in life, these did not disappear while we were playing, and

---

10   Cheating negates the outcome of a game. The world of games, therefore, has a morality and wish: 'May the best person win without cheating and may luck be with him.'

11   Cf. Hamayon, *Jouer*, 138: 'Fiction is always created for there is no play without a context indicating it is play.'

they catch up with us when we stop. And if the players' card table or tennis court constitutes an artificial, abstract space, occupied for the duration of the game, this space-time is embedded in the space-time of social life, which encompasses it, runs through it, overspills it and goes beyond it. Furthermore, it is in the world where work is not a game that the tennis court, footballs, wetsuits and surfboards are produced. In short, the world of games can never be completely separated, detached, from the real world, even where it most differs and is opposed to it.

The imagined imaginary of games is always confronted with a separate reality, which determines the boundaries between the possible and the impossible that impose themselves on both players and the world of games alike. For even if, by making lighter, more robust and more flexible poles, pole-vaulters can now exceed six metres, we already know that no change to the poles will ever enable them to jump forty metres. We can extend the realm of the possible, but we cannot eliminate the impossible. We can only push back the limits. All the impossible things done by Tintin, Kamehameha, in manga or by the *Star Wars* heroes are products of the imagined imaginary, existing only by means of words and drawings, or through special effects. This brings us back to children – this time, not their capacity to imitate the possible, but to imagine the impossible, and to believe in it or not.[12]

We have seen that children know full well that their stuffed bear does not urinate, but they pretend it does. They know in this case that the impossible is not possible. Nevertheless, from somewhere around the age of four, they also begin to believe that the impossible is sometimes possible. A series of experiments has shown that around the age of four, children have understood several of the constraints existing in the world around them, namely:

---

12   Cf. the important work: P. Harris, C. Johnson, K. Rosengren, eds, *Imagining the Impossible: Magic, Scientific and Religious Thinking in Children* (Cambridge: Cambridge University Press, 2000).

- that something cannot be made from nothing;
- that inanimate objects do not move and do not change shape or identity of their own accord; likewise that they do not cease to exist, or disappear, of their own accord;
- that complex processes such as growing up and aging are irreversible.

Thus, children already have concrete experience of several aspects of the world of inanimate objects: their inability to create themselves, their lack of autonomy, their inertia, their permanence, the stability of their shape and identity. And it is only when they are faced, really or imaginarily, with violations of these constraints, already clear for them, that they are going to open their minds to magical or supernatural explanations suggested to them by adults.[13]

The two attitudes – that the impossible is not possible, and that the impossible may sometimes be possible – are not mutually exclusive for children. They refer to different contexts. Children are capable of imagining what would happen if a given constraint that they know by experience was violated. Mountains could walk, they could be punched in two, and so on. The heroes of fairy tales or video games do this regularly, because they have powers not possessed by humans. With a wave of her magic wand, the bad fairy can conjure up a monster that blocks the hero's path, et cetera. All these events are 'counterintuitive'; in other words they take place in an imaginary world that is both like and unlike the world the child has begun to experience and know. But fairy tales and mangas are not invented by children. They are imagined and made to exist by adults. And it is the adults who tell children, when they continue to believe in Santa Claus, that they are now 'too big' to still believe in him. And it is the same adults who, in a Christian family, tell their children each night: 'Don't forget to say your prayers before you go to bed.' What makes it legitimate to tell someone, on the one hand, to stop believing in what you were made to believe, or, on the other hand, to tell them

---

13   Harris, *The Work of the Imagination*, 161–185.

they should go on believing? If it can be done for one, why not for the other? In other words, why not call into doubt a religious belief, or even detach oneself completely from it as in the case of belief in Santa Claus, something just for children? What does it mean to believe?

Two examples can help us illustrate these oppositions. The first is the pleasure we take in watching a magician pull a series of ten white rabbits from a hat or shut a woman in a transparent box, turn the box around and, upon opening it, find it empty. We are fascinated. We know that what we see is not possible, that these are 'illusions', that we should not believe in them. And yet it is hard not to believe that what we saw was 'real', since the rabbits were real rabbits. The second example is that of the miracles that occur at Lourdes or in other holy places. These miracles are authenticated by doctors and by persons who, apart from the beneficiary of the miracle, can attest to them. But the basis of religious beliefs cannot be reduced to testimony of what one has seen. Rather, it lies in the words spoken by Jesus to Thomas who, if he was to believe in Jesus's resurrection, asked to be allowed to place his hand in Jesus's side, to which Jesus replied: 'You believe because you can see me. Happy are those who have not seen and yet believe.'[14]

One last thing needs to be said about games. In Ancient Greece, the Olympic Games had a religious dimension. In Rome, the circus games were designed as much to entertain the gods as the people, and they were organised by the city or funded by rich citizens and therefore associated with power.[15] The games were also rituals, then, which brings us back to the religious imaginary. But, before beginning this new analysis, we must not forget that to play is to embody characters,

---

14 The Gospel according to John, 20:29, *The Jerusalem Bible* (Garden City: Doubleday & Co.).

15 M. Clavel-Levêque, *L'Empire des jeux. Espace symbolique et pratique sociale dans le monde romain* (Paris and Lyon: CNRS, 1984). On the link between shamanism and play, see Hamayon, *Jouer*. Hamayon shows that from the time of Emperor Theodosius, who was the first to ban the Olympic Games (394 CE), the church tried systematically to stamp out games, dancing, etc., which it condemned as diabolical temptations.

make toys or build sandcastles, and so forth. In short, to play is to perform creative acts that often liken those who invent or play games to those who create works of art and to the artists who perform them (musicians, actors, etc.).

CHAPTER SEVEN

Art, or From the Imagined Imaginary to the Materialised Imaginary

Before broaching the problems of the place and role of the imagination in artistic creation, it is crucial to define what we will call here *artistic practices* and to show their extent and universality. By artistic practice, I mean everything people have invented to 'enhance' themselves, to care for their appearance and to introduce 'beauty' into the relations they have produced, not only between themselves and nature, but with the invisible entities whose existence and actions seemed to them to influence their fate: namely, the gods, spirits and the ancestors. This can be found in every era and in all societies, however each may define what it means 'to be beautiful' or 'to make something beautiful'.

It is also essential to see that the domain of the beautiful exceeds in several ways the domain of the arts. When a man from the Baruya tribe in New Guinea picks a flower as he walks through the forest and sticks it in his hair, his gesture is neither a matter of art nor one of ritual. Unlike young children, who do not do it spontaneously, he is enhancing his looks by adding this flower which, furthermore, is not just any flower, since it is yellow, like sunlight, and the sun was the divinity worshipped by the Baruya before their conversion to Christianity. In our own society, think of women who put on makeup before going out and are attentive to what they are going to wear that day. Behind these everyday gestures loom the huge industries of fashion, ready to wear, and the advertising deployed so that this fashion will prevail and therefore sell. Another example, much less noticed, less visible and referring to a reality now nearly vanished, are the city allotments which until recently lined the outskirts of numerous towns and cities. 'Handsome' gardens were those with straight paths, vegetable plots containing a succession of cabbages, carrots, lettuces, et cetera., all growing in straight rows without a weed to be seen. By giving this handsome appearance to his garden, the gardener had put both his garden and himself on display. The pat he would give himself on the back when someone declared that he had a 'fine' garden was not only due to his technical skills or to his knowledge of the plants he grew and their needs in terms of water or fertilizer, but to something else, something more; it was to the care he had taken in organising the space and the plants he cultivated. The peoples of Melanesia, steeped in knowledge of the plants they grow, take care to ensure that their gardens are handsome, and even that they smell good, because beauty and agreeable odours please their ancestors and draw their favour. Beauty and fertility go hand in hand.

Whether it is exercised in a modest form, like choosing a tie to match one's shirt, or in the highly complex technical and ritual forms involved in making a mask in which a spirit will dwell for a time, the aesthetic function is never wholly autonomous. It is always embedded in social relations that recruit it for their own purposes and will therefore invest it with their own meaning. It is present, albeit in very different degrees, in all human beings. For it is not just any African who is capable of taking a piece of wood and carving the statue of a Dogon ancestor, the aspect and dimensions of which are preordained and must be respected. There are, indeed, African and Melanesian artists, even though only a short time ago, many anthropologists and art critics denied their existence because they did not find in the African woodcarver or blacksmith the image of the twentieth-century Western artist, who was released from any allegiance to the representations artists shared with the public, whereas in previous centuries they had depicted the life of Jesus or the Annunciation. For these critics, the African artist was primarily performing a ritual, and he was the anonymous author of his works. Yet the names of African artists and that of their village were known far beyond the borders of their tribe; they were anonymous only because their name was not mentioned, or did not interest the European who bought their work, or, as Michel Leiris confesses to having done, because the latter stole it.[1]

---

1   M. Leiris records this theft in his diary on 6 September 1931, reproduced in M. Leiris, *Phantom Africa*, trans. B. H. Edwards (Calcutta: Seagull Books, 2017 [1934]), 152–154.

But exercise of the aesthetic function overspills the art sphere in yet another way, for since the earliest times, the appreciation of beauty has played a role in human relations with the natural environment. Nature has always presented our senses with its brightly coloured and sweet-smelling flowers, its soft sands, its majestic mountains, with glittering waves rolling and crashing onto a shore, its birdsong and so on.[2] The appreciation of beauty is born of the sensations and emotions aroused by the perception of relations and the order obtaining between forms, between colours, odours, movements, and so forth; and nature presents all that without owing its existence to humans. Artists are not the only ones to feel or seek 'aesthetic' emotions, but they carry this quest the furthest, using their minds and their hands to produce the works that distinguish one society and culture from another and set their mark on the periods of our history. We are going to examine their arts, once again attempting to detect what they have in common, the constants, in spite of their differences.

These differences are easily explained. The arts speak to us through our senses: sight, hearing, smell, touch, and so on; and they thereby differ in the *material* component each has selected *to act* on our senses. These components can be rocks, woods, metals, different colours of clay, plants flexible enough to be braided, or others that produce odours or oils, and even the wind; or again, colours, effects of light, rhythms. All can be used to signify, including the human body itself, which is the supreme support. Thanks to our bodies, we can sing, dance, paint, sculpt, play an instrument, and so forth. And the combination of the senses and the material supports enlisted to signify gives rise to the various arts: music, song, dance, painting, sculpture, the novel, poetry, theatre, ceramics, basketry, weaving, flower arranging, architecture, but also body painting, and more.

A few examples will illustrate the type of 'reality' an artist creates and the effect his or her creations can have on those who view, listen to, touch or read them. My first choice is the novel. A

---

2 Rousseau's 'Profession of Faith of a Savoyard Vicar' is a hymn to the beauties of nature.

novel is the story imagined by an author of a series of events experienced by imaginary characters in a fictional world; it ends in the resolution of something that was at stake between the characters in the story. A novel is made of words and sentences printed on a paper support in the form of a book; reading it is an act that mobilises inner speech in the reader when he silently speaks to himself the words he reads.

The events and the world described in the story thus exist in the beginning only for the author who has imagined it, and then afterwards for each person who reads it. Once the book has been read, the events and the world described no longer exist; but they do not return to nothingness. They continue to have a virtual existence, and they come to life again with each new reader. But each time they come back to life, they are still what they are: 'unreal' social and cultural realities. What does 'unreal' mean? It means that, aside from arousing readers' attention, interest and emotions, the events and characters described in the novel *do not turn into flesh-and-blood characters* living and acting in the *same world* in which the reader lives when not reading the novel. It is this difference that makes the reality of the events and characters present in the novel unreal. This by no means implies that this reality devoid of depth, this unreality, cannot profoundly affect readers, shock them, upset them, or introduce them to other ways of seeing, thinking and even acting.

Everything found in a novel is thus both imagined and imaginary, but the nature and the weight of its imaginary content are not the same in love novels (*The Princess of Cleves*), a historical novel (*War and Peace*), a mystery by Michael Connelly (*The Black Box*) or, finally, a science fiction novel by Asimov. Asimov transports us to a galaxy that does not exist, in spaceships that have yet to be invented, and where humans battle creatures that have nothing human about them but belong to a much more 'advanced' civilisation than our own. From a novel whose author depicts passions between a man and a woman, which are known to exist, to a novel in which the author brings to life creatures without human form living on unknown planets, the work of the imagination required to produced imaginary material is taken further and further. Each time, the nature of the imagined imaginary has a different content and meaning.

But whatever the nature of the novel (even a serial) and however artful the author, everything described – events, characters, outcome – merely attributes feelings, acts, and tragic or happy relations to characters that are the symbols that bear them.[3] Furthermore, all this is expressed and communicated by words, sentences, a style, images, a film, which themselves are symbols. So we see that a novel combines, in its own way, several components: an imagined world that is more or less imaginary while remaining unreal, characters and events charged with symbolic dimensions, all of which is expressed and printed on a material support comprised of the sheets of paper that make up the book.[4] The imagined, the symbolic and the material are the three elements we find, in various forms and proportions, in all art works.

Let us now turn to the example of theatre and the actor playing Hamlet. Sartre writes quite properly: 'The actor who plays Hamlet makes himself, his whole body, serve as an analogon for that imaginary person . . . He uses all his feelings, all his strength, all his gestures as analogons of the feelings and conduct of Hamlet. But by this very fact he irrealizes them. *He lives entirely in an irreal world.* And it matters little that he *really* cries in playing the role' (original emphasis).[5]

To de-realise oneself is to 'act as if' by taking the identification with another much further than does the child who is and is not the teddy bear he plays with and to which he ascribes life. In his *Hamlet*, Shakespeare has combined the three components of the imaginary, the symbolic and elements taken from real life: an unfaithful mother and an accomplice of her lover, who has killed both the man who is her husband and his own brother; a few historical allusions to the

---

3   For instance, Madame Bovary is the figure imagined by Flaubert to represent the provincial petty bourgeoisie, leading their dull lives.

4   Or displayed by an e-book.

5   J.-P. Sartre, *The Imaginary*, 191.

Kingdom of Denmark placed in a fictional setting, and a bloc of pure imaginary: the statue of the Commander, which triggers Hamlet's famous dialogue with himself: 'To be or not to be, that is the question.'[6]

Let us now turn to instrumental music, for instance, Vivaldi's *Four Seasons*. Here there are no words, as in a novel, nor actors on a stage, as in the theatre or the cinema, to communicate the meaning; there are sounds and rhythms produced by the different groups of instruments and musicians that interpret the piece under the direction of a conductor, who imposes his style of execution. Without words, the sounds, timbres and rhythms of the music alone symbolise and communicate to the listener the way Vivaldi experienced and imagined the changing seasons in the surrounding Lombardy countryside when he composed this work, sometime around 1718. In the absence of words, the music will signify something different for each listener, and the signification each gives it is not imposed. The listener draws meaning from the sensations and emotions the music arouses in him or her and which 'evoke' things felt and imagined in the course of his own life. As Lévi-Strauss commented, 'Music has its being in me, and I listen to myself through it.'[7]

In a concert hall, those listening to the music often close their eyes or stare blankly at the musicians and the conductor. We do not listen to a piece of music one note at a time. We listen to it as the synthesis of a whole. And while we are listening, time is as though suspended, or at least is completely one with the living presence of the music as it unfolds. The music is both a real and unreal presence, since once the piece is over the music exists only in the memory and somewhere within the listeners and the musicians. We find in music the same characteristics as in games: creation of a space-time that eclipses the space-time of 'everyday' life, which reasserts itself when the music falls silent, when the concert is over. It is, as Sartre says, like

---

6   On the stage or the screen, we can see Hamlet or Madame Bovary, while when we read Shakespeare's play or Flaubert's novel, we create a mental image of Hamlet or Madame Bovary.

7   C. Lévi-Strauss, *The Raw and the Cooked: Introduction to a Science of Mythology*, vol. 1, trans. J. and D. Weightman (Harmondsworth: Penguin, 1986), 17.

coming out of a dream, leaving an imaginary world that embodied an aesthetic pleasure.[8]

My last example will bring us back to the image, with Leonardo da Vinci's mysterious portrait of the *Mona Lisa*, painted in Florence between 1503 and 1505. The fact that we still do not know the true identity of this woman is of no importance; whoever she was, it is the smile of the woman who is there, looking back at us, that fascinates the millions of visitors to the Louvre. Seen at close range, the painting is nothing but an accumulation of brush strokes that have deposited on the canvas layer upon layer of pigments and oils, which, through the interplay of colours and lines of the body, have created the woman's face and her smile. As with the notes of a musical score, it is not the brushstrokes that the visitor sees from a distance. It is a beautiful, smiling woman who is there, and yet who does not really exist. She is present but in an unreal fashion, present while absent. And yet, this unreal being 'captures' our gaze and 'bewitches' us.

Alfred Gell speaks of alchemy, and even transubstantiation, in the case of the transformation of the oils and pigments that become the *Mona Lisa*.[9] For him, art is a technology of enchantment, and the artist is a sort of magician, like Leonardo da Vinci, who, using the same materials as any other painter of his time, painted a masterpiece that no one else could have produced. For Gell, then, in the first place, it is not a message that an artist wants to transmit; it is this enchantment, this impact on our senses and our emotions, which both captivate and transform us. Detached from its creator, the work becomes a social actor.[10] And it is this same capacity to act on us and to cause us to act that explains the power and effects of sacred objects. We will return to these when we analyse the imaginary of religions. Before

---

8   Sartre, *The Imaginary*, 193. The question of the nature of the 'play acting' in which actors engage was already explored by Diderot in his essay on 'The Paradox of Acting' (1773).

9   A. Gell, 'The Technology of Enchantment and the Enchantment of Technology', in J. Coote and A. Shelton, eds, *Anthropology, Art and Aesthetics* (Oxford: Clarendon Press, 1992), 40–63.

10   A. Gell, *Art and Agency: An Anthropological Theory* (Oxford: Clarendon Press, 1998), 17, 133.

that, however, I will attempt to identify what all forms of art seem to me to have in common, their invariants, as it were.

- Any work of art initially springs from the mind and the sensibility of an individual and thus possesses a mental [*idéel*] and virtual existence that this individual will then transcribe and transform – through a succession of technical and cognitive (and even magical) acts that he has mastered – into a *symbolic* and *material* reality that means something for him and has the potential to arouse in those perceiving it an inextricable mixture of sensations, emotions and representations.

- Because the emotions and meanings with which the artist has imbued his work have been inscribed in it using physical materials that symbolise and communicate these, the meaning the author has given his work can never be completely transparent. Owing to the materiality of its symbolic signifiers, the work both evokes and conceals the meaning it bears, rather than revealing it explicitly. The viewer, the listener or someone who touches it is thereby invited or forced to give it a meaning.

- Because in order to signify and to act, all forms of art make use of physical symbolic materials – chosen by the artist but which differ for each form – the meaning of a work of art for the perceiver must indissolubly go through the senses and the body as well as through the mind.

- Lastly, a work of art, whether secular or sacred, creates a space and a time distinct from those of everyday life. The latter is suspended and eclipsed, as it were, to make way for a time and a space created and occupied by the presence of the work of art and its effect on those who view, listen to or handle it. The presence of the work of art momentarily *de-realises* the world preceding its perception and that which will follow it, and offers in its place, but only for a short time, a virtual world that is and can only be something unreal. Its unreality can be measured and avowed very simply. The *Mona Lisa* will never step down from her frame to become a flesh-and-blood woman. The equestrian statue of Louis

XIV at Versailles will never break into a gallop. The degree of reality of the *un*real makes this impossible. Alternatively, the *un*reality of sacred objects, whether they are works of art or simply tree stumps or rocks, in no way prevents them from enabling the impossible to become possible. Quite the contrary. It is because these objects were made or chosen to host a spirit or a god and have become indispensable to the performance of rituals that they attest to the real existence of a world, this time surreal, that in turn invests them with its presence and power.

Part II

From the Unreal to the Surreal

CHAPTER EIGHT

Concerning the Religious Imaginary

Before going into the domain of believing and beliefs, where, thanks to the human imagination, the impossible is possible, a strong reminder is called for: there exist human realities that can be neither imagined nor felt. It is impossible, for instance, for a sighted person to imagine and feel how someone who has been sightless since birth lives. Likewise, if a person is not deaf, it is impossible for them to imagine and feel how someone who was born deaf lives. Living, for someone who is blind or deaf, means representing to him- or herself others and the world, and interacting in daily life with them. This remark applies to many forms of experiences undergone by those other than oneself, and which remain largely unimaginable and therefore impossible to communicate, such as the inexpressible suffering of the Shoah victims or that of children regularly beaten or raped by their parents.

Before meeting kings and their kingdoms, emperors and their empires, let us first of all step into the world of the gods, spirits and ancestors. We can begin by letting this liturgical poem resonate in us. It was composed in Sumerian in the third millennium before Jesus Christ, and recited or chanted to the glory of the god Enlil, worshipped in Mesopotamia as the ruler of the gods and men:

> Enlil's commands are by far the loftiest,
> his words are holy,
> his utterances are immutable!
> The fate he decides is everlasting,
> his glance makes the mountains anxious,
> his . . . reaches into the interior of the mountains.
> All the gods of the earth bow down to father Enlil,
> who sits comfortably on the holy dais, the lofty engur,
> to Nunamnir, whose lordship and princeship are most perfect.

The Anuna gods enter before him and obey his instructions
   faithfully
The mighty lord, the greatest in heaven and earth,
the knowledgeable judge,
the wise one of wide-ranging wisdom![1]

This is one of the oldest hymns of praise we possess, addressed by humans to one of their gods, stamped in cuneiform characters in clay tablets. Humans had just invented the first known system of writing; they already had kings and lived in cities. And the god they celebrated was also viewed as a king, but one who possessed infinite capacities that even the greatest of kings could not claim, since Enlil is all-knowing, omnipresent and all-powerful, and all the other gods bow down to him as the dignitaries of a kingdom bow before their king. The world of the gods thus reflects the world of humans, and the goings-on there are both like and unlike the goings-on among humans. This is something people know, since their myths tell them so. What, then, is a god or a spirit?

It is a being whose presence is usually imperceptible to our senses but who, depending on the circumstances, can appear in a created or borrowed material form. This being has intentionality, like humans, but also powers that humans normally do not possess. Where does the existence of spirits and gods come from? From the fact that people *believe* they exist. What, then, does it mean to believe?

Believing is the act of proffering representations and judgments, and holding them to be *true*; and because they are true, they come to *invest* the person who believes them, who derives from them the norms and obligations that shape his existence.[2] But to exist is to think, to feel and to act; it is to act upon oneself, to act with (or against) others and on our natural environment.

---

1   The Electronic Text Corpus of Sumerian Literature, Enlil in the E-kur (Enlil A), etcsl.orinst.ox.ac.uk. See also J. Bottéro, *Mésopotamie. L'écriture, la raison et les dieux* (Paris: Gallimard, 1989), 277–278. The key feature of the society of the gods is that it 'sent back an image, 'only better', of the human society even down to its political evolution.

2   On belief, see M. de Certeau, *L'Invention du quotidien*, vol. 1, *Arts de faire* (Paris: UGE, 1980), 299; and P. Ricoeur, 'Croyance' (Paris: Encyclopaedia Britannica. 2002), 810.

But as soon as the existence of spirits and gods is held to be true, and therefore believed in and known, two problems arise for those who believe: the first is to ascertain what those divinities – gods and goddesses, or those less powerful entities such as nature or ancestor spirits – are like; what are the genealogical or other ties between these divinities? For the thousands of years before the invention of writing, and for many human groups or societies that even today have no written language, the source of knowledge about the nature of the gods and their origins lay in the oral narratives that are the founding myths of all religions. I will analyse below the imaginary and symbolic components of myths and from there go on to the definitions proposed by Lévi-Strauss in several passages of his four-volume *Mythology* series.

The second problem confronting believers is how to communicate with their gods and the spirits: how to ensure their presence; how to influence them to fulfil our desires; or how to appease their anger if we have failed to respect, or have trampled on, a taboo they have laid down. Places have to be chosen for that in the natural environment, or edifices erected – temples, mosques, churches – where the gods or God may be encountered on a regular basis. They can also be made present through masks, statues and icons; but we must keep in mind that to make gods or spirits present in man-made objects in no way means to represent them. We will return to this point. But let us begin by examining myths, following for a time, in the steps of Lévi-Strauss.

THE IMAGINARY, THE SYMBOLIC AND THE REAL IN MYTH AND RITUAL

In *The Naked Man*, Lévi-Strauss writes: 'A myth . . . is telling simultaneously on several levels a very different story, for which it has to find a conclusion . . . the simultaneous levels are . . . those of the real, the symbolic and the imaginary.'[3] Every myth is thus the story

---

3   C. Lévi-Strauss, *The Naked Man*, Mythologiques, vol. 4, trans. J. and D. Weightman (Chicago: University of Chicago Press, 1981), 666.

of a series of facts and events that lead to a conclusion: 'The vocabulary [the myths] use relates to three separate categories: the real, the
symbolic and the imaginary. For it is a matter of experience that
there are clinging women and woman-chasers, whereas the cockleburs and the snakelike penises are symbols, and marriage between a
man and a frog or a worm belongs purely to the realm of the
imagination.'[4]

The real present in myths is, therefore, what one can experience
concretely. The symbolic comprises those images, metaphors that
express aspects of the real. And the imaginary is what does not stem
from experience, but from the imagination alone. It is a world that
does not exist as a fact of concrete experience, but in another manner.
Lévi-Strauss emphasises that these three levels, while existing simultaneously in myths, are three separate orders. What is, in fact, the
case, and can we follow him on all these points?

Let us analyse the preceding quotation, which refers to several
very different origin myths. As we have seen, *the real* refers to human
behaviours, to facts that exist *outside* the world of myth. In all societies, there are men who run after women, 'skirt-chasers', and women
who cling to their husband or their lover. To symbolise them, certain
Amerindian myths have given the first a long, retractable, snakelike
penis and have likened the second to cockleburs. Why a snakelike
penis? Because it enables the mythic hero to copulate from a distance
with the women he desires, whether or not they are consenting. And
why cockleburs? Because these have a set of bracts that form a sort of
collar at the base of certain flowers, which grab on to everything that
touches them and make them very hard to remove.

In what myths do these characters appear, in what form, and
what do they do? In the mythology of the North American Indian
peoples, the character with a long penis is Coyote.[5] The coyote is an
animal known for its intelligence and cunning, analogous in that to

---

4   C. Lévi-Strauss, *The Origin of Table Manners*, Mythologiques, vol. 3, trans. J. and
D. Weightman (Chicago: University of Chicago Press, 1990), 84.

5   Lévi-Strauss, *The Naked Man*, 430, myths 697a and 697b, Okanogan.

our European fox. But in the myth, he is something more and something else. He is a demiurge and master of the salmon. The myth tells that one day, at the beginning of time, Coyote was making his way upstream along the riverbank. From time to time, he glimpsed groups of girls on the other bank, to whom he proposed some salmon. If they accepted, he freed the salmon, which henceforth guaranteed the tribes along the river abundant catches of fish. If they refused, Coyote set up obstacles in the river that kept the salmon from spawning in those waters. And in both cases he used his snakelike penis to cross the river and penetrate the girls' vaginas, even if they refused his advances. That is why today the salmon do not come up all the rivers and their tributaries to spawn, but only certain ones.

To understand the allusion to 'clinging women' and to cockleburs, we have to call on other myths. In North America, the Pawnee Indians tell of a clinging woman who changes into a cocklebur.

A man and wife who were being tormented by a voracious she-bear were saved, thanks to a mysterious child who emerged from a clot of buffalo's blood. He killed the she-bear then decided to set out on his travels. One adventure led him to a village where he earned the gratitude of the people. He was offered all the young girls in marriage but none found favour in his eyes. To punish him for his indifference, a woman stuck onto his back and refused to let go. Magic animals came to the hero's aid and tore the woman off in pieces which changed into cockleburs.[6]

To situate Lévi-Strauss's allusion to the marriage between a man and a frog or worm, we must return to South America and to the Ticuna, who have a myth that tells of the marriages of Monmaneki, a great hunter who lived with his mother in the days of the first people who had been fished by the twin demiurges Dyai and Epi. As he hunted, Monmaneki met successively a frog, an arapaço bird, a worm and an macaw. Each time, these female animals changed into a very pretty woman and seduced him. Each time, he married them, but

---

6   Lévi-Strauss, *The Origin of Table Manners*, 72, myth 378, Pawnee.

each time, they left him. Finally, he married an Indian woman like himself. But she turned out to be a strange creature, whose body divided into two sections at the waist and who caught miraculous numbers of fish by entering the water after having left the bottom half of her body on the riverbank. The bone of her spinal column served as a pin to hold the two parts of her body together. One day, Monmaneki's mother was worried because her daughter-in-law had not yet returned, and she went down to the river. There she discovered the bottom section of her body and threw it far away in the belief that she had drowned. When the woman emerged from the river she could not complete herself. Using her arms, she climbed a tree overhanging the bank and later fell onto the back of her husband, who had come looking for her. For days, she clung to him and would not let him eat, but soiled him with her faeces. At length, Monmaneki thought of a trick to get rid of the woman, who turned into a parrot and flew away.[7]

The myth of the clinging woman is thus found in Amazonia, thousands of kilometres south of the Pawnee Indians, who live on the Great Plains of North America. In another major cycle of North American myths, the cycle known as the wives of the heavenly bodies Sun and Moon, two brothers, both of whom are demiurges, are pondering the best wife for them. Moon chooses a pretty Indian woman; Sun, a frog, because she does not screw up her face like women do when they look at him. At the home of their husbands' mother, the frog-wife drools, is incapable of helping her mother-in-law around the house and is mocked daily by her brother-in-law, Moon, who is proud of his pretty Indian wife whose conduct fully satisfies her mother-in-law. One day, at her wit's end, the frog-wife jumps onto Moon and will not let go. This is why, the Indians say, we see spots on the face of the Moon.[8] The conclusion of the story thus gives the 'explanation' of an

---

7   Ibid., 25–26, myth 354, Tikuna.
8   Ibid., 57–58, myth 369, Assiniboine; 58–59, myth 370, Wichita; 207–209, myths 425 and 426, Arapaho.

astronomical phenomenon by relating its 'origin'. This is the etio-logical content of the myth.[9]

Based on this sparse mythic material, can we verify whether the three components of the myth singled out by Lévi-Strauss – the real, the symbolic and the imaginary – are, as he affirmed, 'separate levels'? Let us take the example of Coyote. The 'real' coyote is an animal that runs and hunts on the Great Plains. The Indians knew his features and physical capacities, as well as his ways and habits. As a real animal, coyote leads his life independently, unaware of what the Indians have made him in their myths and rituals. But when Coyote enters their mythology, he does so stripped of most of his real attributes, with the exception of his intelligence and his cunning. He enters, then, not as a wild coyote, but as the animal-symbol of a few features he shares with humans. Furthermore, he enters mythology endowed with a snakelike penis that allows him to copulate from the far bank of rivers with women who accept (or not) his advances. This imaginary organ de-realises the animal-symbol even further and definitively takes Coyote out of the world of familiar realities that can be empirically verified in the ordinary course of life.[10]

But at the same time, owing to its monstrous proportions, this imaginary penis transforms Coyote into a symbol of a particular cate-gory of men found in all societies, skirt-chasers with an insatiable sexual appetite. Coyote represents these men. Thus, by his intelli-gence, his cunning, his sexual organ and his appetite for women, Coyote is both an imaginary and a symbolic character, but he is

---

9 Cf. Ibid., 228: 'But what is true of the rules of kinship is also valid for mythic narratives. Neither are limited to being simply what they *are*: *they serve a purpose* – to solve problems which are sociological in the one case and socio-logical in the other.' This affirma-tion contradicts the sensational declaration made at the beginning of *The Raw and the Cooked* (p. 10): 'Mythology has no obvious practical function.'

10 We must remember that several different 'objects' or 'situations' can symbolise the same thing or that the same symbols can symbolise different realities. For instance, in Amerindian mythology the pair Sun and Moon can symbolise an elder and a younger brother, twin brothers, a man and woman, a husband and his wife, a father and mother, and so on. Hence the potential polysemous and ambiguous nature of the meaning of many symbols.

conceived and constructed in the image of humans; he is an anthropomorphic being.

This anthropomorphic being is neither animal nor human. He is a demiurge, a supernatural being who commands the salmon people and who one day decides to proceed upstream, following the banks of the rivers flowing into the Pacific Ocean, causing thousands of salmon to follow him. On his way, he encounters women from the tribes living along the rivers and, depending on whether or not they accept his offers of salmon and sex, frees or does not free the fish to swim up the waters of their river. The result is that certain tribes can both fish and hunt, while the rest must be content to hunt and eat the meat of their game animals.

So, Coyote-demiurge is much more than Coyote, animal-symbol of cunning, or Coyote, animal-symbol of women-loving men. This time, he is a purely imaginary being, whose existence does not refer to any empirical experience that might invalidate him, but whose mythic actions are totally counterintuitive. What ties did the Indians discover between the real coyote, an animal living in the prairies, and real salmon, fish living in the Pacific Ocean that swim up certain rivers each year to spawn?

As a demiurge, Coyote functions in this case as the symbol of the existence and powers of (usually invisible) beings capable of commanding the forces and elements of the universe and, therefore, able to act on the fate of human beings. Coyote has become a 'metaphysical' animal, an unreal creature that symbolises the existence of a 'surreal world' populated by all manner of benevolent and malevolent gods and spirits, who make up the religious world of the American Indians and to whom they address their rituals. We therefore understand why myths are not supposed to have an author, or at least not a human author. They are said to have been transmitted directly to the ancestors at the time of the first people, who then passed them down from one generation to the next, until our day. Or, it is said that the gods inspired a shaman, who then revealed the myths to the members of his tribe or clan. In short, myths come from somewhere beyond the world of humans and belong to the realm of the sacred.

Coyote-demiurge does not exist, any more than does Coyote of the snakelike penis, outside the fictional world described by the myths. But he nevertheless exists fully, both subjectively and socially, for those who believe in the existence of entities we call gods or spirits. This belief is always an act of faith in the existence of a (usually invisible) reality that mirrors and underpins visible reality. It is in this invisible part of the real that what is impossible in the visible world becomes possible. Such a mental process is not restricted to Amerindian religions, though. It is an invariant of all religions. All entail a mental act that transforms a belief into truth, positing and causing it to be experienced as true.

What, then, is the mental process, the act of faith underpinning the Amerindian world of myth and ritual? It is the postulate that, in the beginning, humans, animals and even plants were not different from one another. The purpose of myths is thus to expose the way things were in the beginning, and what happened to make the world the way it is today, where coyotes no longer have a snakelike penis, men no longer marry worms or frogs, and so on.

Let us take a few myths at random. In one myth, a jaguar removes its skin and assumes human shape.[11] In another myth, an exasperated human changes into a stingray.[12] Or a girl offers herself in marriage to Porcupine, in order to have a constant supply of the best quills with which to decorate her husband's clothing.[13] At that time, plants, too, were personal beings. The frond of a palm tree changes into a man married by two women.[14] In another myth, a woman marries a root and gives birth to a demiurge.[15] In yet another, a woman marries the spirit master of wild pigs,[16] and so forth. In fact, the divinities themselves can take on a human or an animal form, and sometimes even

---

11   Lévi-Strauss, *The Raw and the Cooked*, 125, myth 53, Tikuna.

12   C. Lévi-Strauss, *From Honey to Ashes, Introduction to a Science of Mythology*, Mythologiques, vol. 2, trans. J. and D. Weightman (Chicago: University of Chicago Press, 1973), 309n19, myth 292b, Bororo.

13   Ibid., 248–249, myth 445, Arapaho.

14   Ibid., 180–184, myth 241, Warao.

15   Ibid., 442, cycle of Shuswap, Lilloet myths, etc.

16   Ibid., 443, myth 17, Warao.

the form of a plant, such as the Spirit of Tobacco, a plant that enables communication with the gods. Moon marries a beautiful Indian woman, but his brother, Sun, prefers to marry a frog. In short, in this world of myth, there is no watertight division between living beings, humans and the gods. And this religious universe was present and active in the Indians' everyday lives through the succession of rituals they celebrated over the course of the seasons to bring back the rain, or so that the buffalo would return each year to 'darken the plains', or for a good maize harvest, granted by Old Woman Who Never Dies (mistress of maize), and so on.

If we compare this metaphysical universe with that of the major religions of salvation (Christianity, Islam) or of deliverance (Hinduism, Buddhism), a fundamental difference becomes clear. Whereas religions of salvation and deliverance are primarily forward looking, turned towards an afterlife, Amerindian religion is turned towards primordial times, a time before the separation of the species (including humans) that existed in the natural environment, a separation due to supernatural causes and beings. But this separation did not break all the ties that originally united humans, animals and plants. Humankind must and can continue to communicate with the spirits controlling the natural elements. But it can no longer do this directly and in an informal setting. It must be done ritually and, most often, by a shaman whose spirit can travel to the spirit world, or by a priest who knows the rituals and liturgy required for their worship. We therefore understand why one of the major problems Indian myths try to explain is that of the theft of fire from the Sky People by humans, a theft that enabled people to no longer have to eat their food raw, like animals, but to be able to cook it.[17] Obviously, fire from the sky is opposed to water from the sky, rain; the hero who is indifferent to women is opposed to Coyote the woman chaser; and so forth. The universe of myth contains and explains all oppositions.

---

17   Hence the title of the first volume in the Mythologiques series, *The Raw and the Cooked*. For the theme of the theft of fire, see the conclusion to the fourth volume in the series, *The Naked Man*, 625–695.

Are we therefore justified in affirming that in myth, the real, the symbolic and the imaginary are three separate levels? I cannot follow Lévi-Strauss on this point. The three components of myths are distinct, but inseparable. Coyote's snakelike penis is *imaginary*, but at the same time, its length and the use to which it is put make it the symbol of the male skirt-chaser. And Coyote is a demiurge only because he commands the salmon, and therefore because he possesses an imaginary power. This power makes him the analogue of all the entities that command the elements and the forces of nature. Finally, what is real in the myth of the adventures of Coyote? Merely allusions to facts, situations, realities that exist outside the world of myth and are de-realised and made unreal by mythic thought. Coyote has become a mytheme, a component of mythic discourse. His name no longer has the same meaning as it does in the language of ordinary life or hunting; it is loaded with new meanings, both figurative and meta-phorical, which makes myths a metalanguage that produces meaning by pointing up imaginary analogical relations between beings and aspects of the universe that have themselves been turned into symbols. For it is not only the characters of the myths that are imaginary and symbolic; it is the whole story of their adventures, the myth with all its variants. The characters of the myths are operators of actions, but they enact their powers only because they are set in motion by a schema that organises their actions and subjects them to its logic. A mythic schema is the imaginary mechanism that sets the characters of the myth in motion and features them in adventures that end in an expected or unexpected way. The mythic schema of Coyote's adven-tures is his trip upriver and his offers of salmon and sex to women who, depending on their answers, will prompt him to grant or refuse the presence of salmon to the tribes living along the rivers to which these women belong.

Another important mythic schema in North American Indian mythology is the canoe trip of Sun and Moon, two brothers, two demi-urges who travel, one (Moon) at the front, to paddle, the other (Sun) at the back, to steer. Both will have to remain in the right place and at the right distance apart in order not to upset the craft during the trip. From the outset, the myth thus combines imaginary realities (the two demi-urges) and components taken from reality outside the myths (taking care to stay at the right distance to paddle and steer a canoe in order not to upset it). The canoe trip will thus act as a schema to bring together, through a series of analogies, various aspects of nature and life in society. For example: What is the right distance for a man and a woman to be able to marry? The mythic schema will show that they must be neither too close together, brother and sister for example, for fear of committing incest, nor too far apart, as in the union of a man and a female animal or vice versa. The canoe trip also makes it possible to conceive the distance the sun must maintain in order not to scorch the earth and its inhabitants, or why, for the same distance, the downriver canoe trip takes much less time than going upriver. In this case, mythic thought imagines that in the beginning this was not the case, but that the demiurge 'decided that the waters of the river would flow downstream and the salmon would swim upstream'.[18] Sun and Moon's round trip can also be used to think the alternation between day and night, or the relative inequality of day and night depending on the seasons, and so on.

When listening to the myths, the Indians can thus hear several messages at once: the explicit, patent content, that of the story's conclusion; but also a number of other messages, this time latent, present in the interplay of the analogies used and which they alone can grasp because, whether unconsciously or consciously, they are able to decipher them. Myths are thought that calls for thought. They are not fairy tales, nor are they stories to delight or frighten children. They are narratives that claim to give individuals access to a *supra-reality* that has been present since the beginning of humanity which does not reveal itself to everyone but only to certain persons. Mythic narratives thus deal in truths, in beliefs that are to be received and experienced as true. Humankind would not have invented hundreds of thousands of myths over the millennia if no one were going to believe them. To believe in them means to believe they are true and

18   Lévi-Strauss, *The Origin of Table Manners*, 172; Yurok myth. We find the same theme in the myths of many Pacific Coast tribes.

therefore to act on oneself, on others and on the world according to their truth: this is the crux of mythico-religious thought. Myths are the primordial components of all religions and are also present, but in other forms, in all political systems.

It is here that we find a flaw, with crucial consequences, in Lévi-Strauss's analysis of myth and ritual. The problem is not the 'structural' analysis of myths. This method is essential to discover the structures immanent to the different transformations of the versions of a myth, or group of myths. And it is just as indispensable to anthropologists wanting to study kinship systems, and to linguists attempting to identify the phonetic and syntactic structures of the thousands of languages still spoken today.

Nor is it the fact that, having revealed the existence of the three components of myths – the real, the symbolic and the imaginary – Lévi-Strauss stopped there, without further analysis, having posited them as belonging to three separate levels, even though they are clearly distinct but inseparable. Coyote's snakelike penis is imaginary, and at the same time it is the symbol of the skirt-chaser. Furthermore, Lévi-Strauss did not ask what this mythic reality retained of the reality existing outside myths.[19] Yet the distinction between the three levels sufficed for him to take on the huge task of analysing the structures, themes and schemata of 813 myths, and as many variants from the mythology of the Indians of South and North America, which he had chosen from the thousands of other myths in view of following the transformations of the Bird Nester myth. This particular myth is told by the Bororo of South America. It opens *The Raw and the Cooked*, and its variants take us to the close of the final volume of the *Mythology* series and the myths concerning the theft of heavenly fire

---

19   Lévi-Strauss simply stated it, but in a strange way, for he implied that by means of metaphor, the real became first symbolic and then imaginary, before being implemented through schemata of mythic thought; whereas it is the imaginary that manufactures symbols using elements taken from realities existing independently of myth. 'The other axis, which is specifically that of myth, is related rather to the category of metaphor; it . . . oblig[es] the concrete data to cross the successive, discontinuous thresholds separating the empirical order from the symbolic order, then from the order of the imagination, and lastly from schematism' (*The Naked Man*, 679).

by the earth people; these myths are found in the far Pacific Northwest, among the coastal Salish and Sahaptin.[20]

The imaginary of Amerindian mythology contains a religious universe based on a metaphysical postulate, which I summed up earlier as follows: In the beginning, humans, animals and plants were not different from one another, and among them lived spirits and gods who could take on human or animal form at will. Humans could copulate with or marry animals or plants and even, in some cases, become demiurges themselves. Following a series of events provoked by beings with supernatural powers, the world became what it is today; the different species are now separate and have assumed their present-day forms, but they have retained something of what they shared in the beginning. In this way, some humans – shamans, priests or others – guided by the spirits or by the gods, are still able to communicate with them with the aid of prayers and rituals.

This premise of the truth of the myths, posited by an act of faith shared by the Indian peoples, is in fact the reason for the multiple rites and rituals invented by these tribes to communicate with the Sun, the Moon, the Thunder, the gods of the winds and the rain, with the Spirit Master of the Buffalo, with Old Woman Who Never Dies, associated with the goddess Moon and who commands the maize, and so forth. Yet Lévi-Strauss affirms: 'The truth of the myth does not lie in any special content. It consists in logical relations that are devoid of content.'[21] It is hard, in this case, to give a meaning to ritual, which becomes for Lévi-Strauss, 'a bastardization of thought, brought about by the constraints of life . . . [an] attempt to re-establish the continuity of lived experience, segmented through the schematism by which mythic speculation has replaced it'.[22] This series of affirmations about myths, and especially about the nature of ritual, is the flaw in his analysis that limits its theoretical scope.[23] Lévi-Strauss justified his

---

20   Lévi-Strauss, *The Naked Man*, 418, 618–619.
21   Lévi-Strauss, *The Raw and the Cooked*, 240.
22   Lévi-Strauss, *The Naked Man*, 675.
23   Concerning this flaw, see my analysis of the work of Lévi-Strauss in *Lévi-Strauss*, trans. N. Scott (London and New York: Verso, 2018), 246–447.

assertions, pretexting 'the contradiction inherent in the human condition, between two inevitable obligations: living and thinking.'[24]

But ritual does not oppose living and thinking. It combines acting with thinking, and the union of thought and action is precisely what living is. Myths are an interpretation of the world, but as stories they do not act directly on it. Only rituals transform mythico-religious thought into collective or individual actions. Thinking for the pleasure of thinking is not the fundamental reason for myths. Only ritual can transform the imaginary truths of myths into corporeally experienced, embodied truths.[25] And it is because these imaginary truths run counter to intuition that the stories told in myths can appear as revelations made to our ancestors by spirits or gods. It is also because the human mind has always been able to oppose raw and cooked, hot and cold, sky and earth, et cetera, that we find the same mythic schemata and the same imaginary explanations in myths from very different societies that have never come in contact with each other. There is no mystery in that. But because, until today, it is indeed men who ceaselessly invent new myths and not the myths which invent themselves, it is impossible to subscribe to Lévi-Strauss's flamboyant affirmation that has intimidated more than one reader:

I therefore claim to show, not how men think in myths, but how myths operate in men's mind [*les mythes se pensent*; literally: myths think themselves] without their being aware of the fact. And, as I have already suggested, it would perhaps be better to go still farther and, disregarding the thinking subject completely, proceed as if the

---

24   Lévi-Strauss, *The Naked Man*, 681.

25   Victor Turner had reproached Lévi-Strauss for this in his book *The Ritual Process: Structure and Anti-Structure* (Chicago: Aldine, 1969), 43: 'The whole person and not just the mind . . . is existentially involved in life and death issues.' To which Lévi-Strauss responded sarcastically: 'This may well be so, but when it has been said, and pious lip service has been paid to the importance of the emotions, we have not advanced one step nearer to an explanation of how the strange activities characteristic of ritual . . . can produce such fine results' (*The Naked Man*, 668).

thinking process were taking place in the myths, in their reflection upon themselves and in their interrelation.[26]

That mythic thinking occurs in each of us, each time we imagine a world in which the impossible is not only thinkable but possible, is clear and can be verified, but that in no way proves that the thinking process took place in the myths through our intermediary. It is clear that the impossible is thinkable,[27] but to posit that the impossible is possible requires us to take another step, a leap even, which is performed by 'faith' in the truth of what is said or written, of what we hear or read.

Without these acts of faith, how could we understand how imaginary mental realities became temples, rituals, institutions, social groups specialised in the worship of the gods, priests; and how they finally became symbolic and material social realities, and individual and collective social practices?

Let us now turn to the second problem confronting those who believe in the existence of spirits and gods.

COMMUNICATING WITH SPIRITS AND GODS

For those who believe in their existence, how are spirits and gods going to manifest their presence? How can we persuade them to serve our desires? How can we appease their wrath if we have been disrespectful to them or have trampled a taboo they have prescribed? To be sure, they can make an occasional appearance or give a sign of their presence and their action by miracles, by the sudden, unexpected flight of a bird, by a gust of wind. Of course, only a believer can grasp and understand these signs, which act as symbols. But believers also need to experience the presence of the spirits and the gods in which they believe in a less sporadic and unpredictable, and more

---

26   Lévi-Strauss, *The Raw and the Cooked*, 12; my emphasis.

27   Science fiction novels or films are a commonplace proof; for example: *Star Wars, Terminator*, etc.

permanent and stable, manner. They do this by choosing and adapting places where, more or less regularly, they come to seek their presence and where this presence can be manifested in a tree standing in the forest, or through man-made objects – statues, masks combined with invocations, offerings or sacrifices that are part of the rituals entailed in their worship.

Let us take the case of masks, statues, paintings, icons, et cetera made to render the presence of the spirits and the gods. To render the presence of a spirit or a god in a statue or a mask does not mean to represent them; it means 'to presentify' them, make them present, offer them a container where they may be encountered, where they will come to listen to us each time we address them, ritually or informally. By 'ritually', I mean according to an established code that imposes certain words, postures, gestures (genuflection, prostration, bowing of the head, silence; or on the contrary, songs, chants and trances) and so forth. A spirit can also manifest itself to humans by taking possession of the body of one of their numbers, who then serves as a medium through whom to communicate with the others. But conversely, one of the humans who has the power can send his spirit out to encounter malevolent entities who have taken away, in view of devouring it, the spirit of a woman, for instance, who then becomes nothing but a 'soul-less' body, who withers away before their eyes. The capacity to do this is the privilege of shamans or exorcists. Thus, to presentify is not the same thing as to represent, and that is the difference between a consecrated icon or an African sculpture 'loaded' with the presence and the power of a spirit, and the painting of the *Mona Lisa*. The *Mona Lisa* represents a lovely woman with an enigmatic, fascinating smile, who probably existed. But those who see and admire her know intuitively that this woman is both present as an image and absent as a person, and that this absence makes her presence an unreal reality.

This is far different from the perception of the presence of a spirit in a mask made secretly in the depths of the forest, or in such objects as certain Bambara boli, to which the kings would offer human sacrifices when preparing to go to war or when they returned victorious.

According to the definition proposed by Youssouf Cissé, who had the opportunity to study them, a boli is 'the manifestation and emanation of the energy, of the life force of a divinised spirit for which it serves as a dwelling, a container'. There are other sorts of boli as well, boli that make it rain and ensure a good harvest, boli to bring death, or to predict the future. Prayers and offerings are made to these boli, but no human sacrifices. The boli are made by someone who is 'pure', who fashions them from different kinds of clay, powdered organic materials and special strips of cloth that symbolise the Milky Way and are linked to the 'multiplication of things and beings'. When they have been made, dogs or rams are sacrificed, and their blood smeared on the body of the boli to keep it alive. The 'internal' nature of the boli thus depends on the nature of the materials used, on the god named during its making and the prayers said in order to mobilise the life-force of this god or spirit.[28]

Fed and showered with libations, honoured with songs, chants and dances, the god has no choice but to be attentive to the humans who strive to bring him close and dispose him to answer their prayers. Sometimes, however, as in the ancient kingdom of Zaire or in certain contemporary Afro-Cuban religions, once the spirit has come into a statuette, it is no longer free to leave and finds itself prisoner of a human master and forced to obey him.[29]

The same relation of reciprocity and power between humans and the spirits they worship, and whose presence they suppose in the objects they have made to incarnate them, appeared in spectacular fashion in the Western Christian High Middle Ages. These relations manifested themselves in what is known as the ritual of the 'humiliation of the saints', which was performed when they seemed no longer to protect and answer those who worshipped them.

The saints were present in churches in the form of relics of early Christian martyrs or persons sanctified by the church, but also in the

---

28   Y. T. Cissé, in C. Falgarettes-Leveau, ed., *Magies* (Paris: Éditions Dapper), 149. See also E. Dianteill, 'Le Pouvoir des objets. Culture matérielle et religion en Afrique et en Haïti', *Annales des Sciences Sociales des Religions*, 110 (2000), 29–40.

29   Dianteill, 'Le Pouvoir des objets', 33.

form of statues whose eyes and gaze were exaggerated.[30] Humiliating the saint consisted in placing the relics on the floor of the church or on the ground and covering them with thorns. The doors of the church were then closed, preventing the celebration of the mass and other liturgical acts. Veneration of the saint and all other liturgical acts were thus suspended until the community of the faithful decided that the saint had heard them and corrected his or her attitude. The retaliatory measures then ceased, and the relics were put back in their usual place to the sound of joyful singing.[31]

Medieval religious practices with respect to saints and their worshippers resemble, in many ways, our description of Bambara relations with the spirits present in the sacred objects they themselves made in order to secure the presence of the spirits they worshipped. The medieval tradition was a contractual relation and therefore included the possibility of relations of power and forms of reciprocal coercion between the saints and humans. Devotees could always fear that the saint would punish them for their lack of fervour and their misconduct. But they also knew that they could retaliate by lowering their saints if these failed in their obligations. In the mind of believers, there was thus the idea of a reciprocal relation between the intensity with which they worshipped their saints and the number and importance of the benefits and protection they were supposed to provide in return. This intensity was measured by the number of tapers and ex-votos, the richness of the ritual trappings surrounding the relics (in their reliquary) or the saint's statue.

Writing on European statues in the Middle Ages, R. W. Scribner explains that vision was considered to establish a reciprocal relation between the viewer and object viewed.[32] Therefore, when in the

---

30   P. Brown, *The Cult of the Saints: Its Rise and Function in Latin Christianity* (Chicago: University of Chicago Press, 1981). Brown is quoting the Latin funerary inscription on the tomb of Saint Martin of Tours (end 6th century CE): 'Here lies Martin the bishop, of holy memory, whose soul is in the hand of God; but he is fully here, present and made plain in miracles of every kind.'

31   P. Geary, 'L'Humiliation des Saints', *Annales ESC* 34, n° 1 (1979), 27–42.

32   R. W. Scribner, ed., *Bilder und Bildersturm im Spätmittelalter und in der früher Neuzeit* (Wiesbaden: Harrassowitz, 1990), 19.

course of their devotions the faithful would gaze at the relics, the image or the statue of their saint, the sacred force of the latter was transmitted to the worshippers. But this force became effective only through the believers' inner attitude, the intensity and purity of their faith, and their upstanding behaviour. The humiliation of the saints was ultimately condemned by the Church in 1274, at the Second Council of Lyon, where it was declared that the Church no longer tolerated the people reprimanding saints and other supernatural powers and their interruption of liturgical obligations in order to do so. In 1215 the Lateran Council had already forbidden priests to continue to bless ordeals, a very old judicial ritual that had been assimilated to a divine judgment and that had gained considerable importance in the Middle Ages. As the Gregorian reform was implemented, the Christian notion of holiness progressively took on a different meaning in the Western Roman Catholic Church.[33] The same did not apply, however, to the Orthodox Church, and the reciprocal relation between the faithful and their favourite icons endures today, despite the few decades during which the Byzantine emperors decided to destroy the icons and forbid their veneration.[34]

Lastly, let us note that the presentification of a spirit or a god does not necessarily imply a human or animal figuration of this spirit.[35] Bones or stones can manifest this presence just as well, for those capable of perceiving it.[36] The oldest representations of divinities in archaic Greece were more or less rough-hewn wooden idols in the form of pillars or posts, called 'xoana'. Jean-Pierre Vernant tells us that these idols were the object of ritual operations. They were bathed,

---

33   J. P. Genet, 'Légitimation religieuse et pouvoir dans l'Europe médiévale latine', in *Rome et l'État Moderne européen* (Rome: École Française de Rome, 2007), 387–388. See also P. Brown, *Society and the Holy in Late Antiquity* (Berkeley: University of California Press, 1982), 222–250 and *The Cult of the Saints*.

34   G. P. Marshal, 'Jalons pour une histoire de l'iconoclasme au moyen-âge', *Annales, HSS* 5 (1995), 1135–1156.

35   In Ancient Egypt, Horus, god of the Sky, the Sun and the Moon, was represented as a falcon, a sacred bird. Cf. D. Meek, *Les Dieux égyptiens* (Paris: Hachette, 1993).

36   Hence the importance for Christians of relics of the saints and martyrs.

dressed and undressed. They were fed. They were often considered to have been fashioned and given to a chiefly or priestly family by a divinity, which enhanced the family's prestige and its power over others. Vernant cites as an example of a sacred object Agamemnon's sceptre, which was believed to have been made by the fire god, Hephaestos, and given by Zeus to Hermes, who then gave it to the Atrides and finally to Agamemnon, who held it at the time of the Trojan War.

Later, in the era of the Athenian city-state, figuration of the gods would undergo a fundamental mutation. The gods would be represented in the form of extremely handsome male and female bodies, and their statues would be placed on public view in their temples.[37] The xoana of archaic Greece can be compared to the central house post of the Kafika clan chief, the most important from the standpoint of ritual duties of the four clans that made up the population of the Polynesian island of Tikopia. The chief was the direct descendant of the island's protector god. But before dying and becoming a god, this ancestor was the man who had managed to convince the different incoming groups vying for possession of the territory to cease fighting and to cooperate, in both ritual and material matters. Which they did. But once peace had been restored, one of the chiefs who had been won over, jealous of the man's prestige, murdered him. Thereupon, the major gods of the Polynesian pantheon made the slain man the atua, the god of the island of Tikopia, whose descendants were to occupy the most important functions in the annual cycle of cosmological rites, ensuring the reproduction of natural species, and success in fishing the seas and farming the land.

Raymond Firth attended these rituals during his first fieldwork, in 1928. He describes how Chief Ariki Kafika invoked the island's god by rubbing the centre post of the temple with his hands, explaining to the anthropologist that he knew the god was present when he called

37   J. P. Vernant, 'De la présentification de l'invisible à l'imitation de l'apparence', lecture at the École du Louvre, 1983; reproduced in *Entre mythe et politique* (Paris: Seuil, 1996), 356–377.

upon him, but that he also knew that the god's presence in no way took the form of this post.[38] The post was merely the physical object to which to address physical acts of veneration, 'which the god himself could observe in spiritual invisible form from elsewhere'.[39]

The presentification of a spirit or a god in a physical form, whether or not it was man made, thus has nothing in common with the manner in which a doll or the *Mona Lisa* is present. Both the toy and the portrait render the presence of beings who remain absent in their presence, whereas this is not the case for objects that presentify spirits or gods. The latter are present in their very absence.

Once the sacred objects have been created or chosen, once the rituals have been performed to make the spirits present in them, humans know that they are there, but they also know that the gods, having heard their prayers, may not care to listen to them or fulfil their desires. They also know that even though they themselves made the objects that will receive the spirits they are invoking, they are not the ones who created the gods, nor those who imagined the existence of the spirits. For the men who spend months deep in the forest, far from the eyes of women and noninitiates, making the superb Sulka masks so admired by André Breton, the spirits' presence in their masks owes not to the men's artistic talents but to the fact that when they make them, by means of their rituals and invocations, their own spirit and gestures have already been magically 'enchanted' by the spirit that is going to dwell in the mask.[40]

To presentify is therefore not the same as to represent; and for the religions that think there is only one god and that this god cannot be represented – which is the case of Judaism and Islam – any

---

38   R. Firth, *The Work of the Gods in Tikopia* (London: Athlone, 1967), 209–211, 218–220, 234, 245; *Symbols: Public and Private* (London: Oxford, Allen & Unwin, 1973), 26, 175.

39   Firth, *Symbols*, 175.

40   In his famous *Argonauts of the Western Pacific* (London: Routledge, 1922), B. Malinowski had written that for Trobrianders who practiced *kula* exchanges with the other islands, the magical power contained in the carved bow figures of their big canoes caused their partners to lose their capacity to negotiate and led them to easily yield their most beautiful arm and neckbands to their kula exchange partners.

representation of God is both needless and blasphemous. Hence what is known as the iconoclasm quarrel, set off when the Byzantine emperors in the eighth and ninth centuries CE opposed the veneration of holy images and ordered their destruction (in Greek, *klao* means to break). It is significant too that today, Africans who sell masks or statues to foreigners perform a ritual that 'discharges' their sacred energy before letting them go. Having been disenchanted, the object becomes simply a statue or a mask to be displayed in a museum or living room. It has become a decorative piece of 'African art', of interest to specialists and art lovers for a variety of reasons. But it is also an object that has come into the market of exotic or 'primitive' art to become a commodity that is more or less expensive. Other imaginaries, those of collectors or museum curators, then take over from the imaginary that had given rise to the work in Africa and made it a sacred object.

Another way to bring to light the imaginary of religions is to study representations of death and the fate of humans when they die. We can show that all religions, whether they are polytheistic, monotheistic, tribal or universal, share one presupposition: namely, that death is not the end of life, that after death the deceased begins another life, in another form, and travels to the world beyond imagined by their religion. Of course, when someone is dying and then dies, those present at the death do not 'see' one or several souls leave the body. They have a body they must dispose of in a socially prescribed form (burial, cremation, exposition of the corpse, etc.) before beginning the process of mourning the 'departed'. In short, in all religions, *death is not the opposite of life, but of birth*. Death sunders that which birth had joined.

A human is not born solely as a result of the sexual relations between the man and the woman who engendered him or her. For the foetus created by these relations – whatever the role attributed in this creation to the man's semen or the woman's menstrual blood – to become a real child, one or more souls or spirits must enter into it and the body become 'animated'. This spirit can be that of an ancestor who wants to come back to life and therefore incarnates him- or herself in a descendant. Or it can be a soul created by God and introduced by him when he wishes, and in the form he desires, into the body of the child, as Hildegard of Bingen so well described in the twelfth century CE in her *Liber Scivias*. This nun was a great German mystic who had had the vision of this Christian mystery in the form of a ball of fire introduced by the Holy Spirit into the body of a child while still in its mother's womb.[41] But once this soul has taken flesh, it immediately finds itself stained by the original sin committed by Adam and Eve, the couple created by God and the ancestors of all humankind. This sin is then transmitted down through the generations to the children born of carnal relations between their parents. The child must therefore be baptised at birth, to cleanse its soul of this sin and so that it will be judged on the last day only for the sins committed during its own lifetime. But, if all religions invariably postulate that the deceased continues to live after death and travels to the dwelling place of the dead, only certain religions add another postulate: namely, that the deceased will be judged for the acts they committed in life; and that when they die, they will face a judgment rendered by God or the gods.

The example of the Fore, a group of tribes living in the New Guinea Highlands, will serve to illustrate the case of religions that imagine a life after death that does not entail the idea of a postmortem judgment of the dead. The Fore are well known in anthropology and medicine: in anthropology, because the deceased members of these tribes were consumed by groups of the deceased's female kin or affines; in medicine, because a fatal neurodegenerative disorder, known as kuru, is found in this population and is probably linked to the eating of cadavers, since it affects primarily women. The discovery of this disorder and its study earned Daniel Carleton Gajdusek and E. Richard Sorenson the Nobel Prize in medicine. This was the beginning of the discovery of prion diseases, which include the now-famous 'mad cow' disease.

---

41 Hildegard of Bingen, *Scivias* (Mahwah, NJ: Paulist Press, 1990); see also J.-C. Schmitt, 'La mort dans le moyen-âge chrétien', in M. Godelier, ed., *La mort et ses au-delà* (Paris: CNRS, 2014), 179–201.

To understand the meaning of the Fore mortuary rites, we must begin with Fore cosmology and its connections with their representations of the components of the human person, who for them is an integral part of this cosmos.[42] The Fore believe that the earth has always existed and is called Bagina. The rivers are his blood, the rocks his bones, the ground his skin and all the plants his hair. One day Bagina, in the form of an old man, created the ancestors of all the Fore clans, each time in the form of one man and one woman per clan. He did this in a sacred place present in the landscape, Andai. When he had finished, Bagina reverted to the earth of which the Fore's ancestors (the Amani) became the custodians, and it is now through them that their descendants interact with Bagina's hidden powers. Every day the landscape surrounding the Fore attests to the truth of what is for us their mythology.

The Fore believe that every human being is born with three souls, each associated with a body humour. These souls must be reunited after the death of the person, who will then become an ancestor living in the land of the dead, Kwelanamandi, a place quite similar to the earth where humans live, but where war, famine, sorcery and so forth no longer exist and which is a very pleasant place to continue one's life. Of these three souls, the first (*auma*), distinguishes one individual from the another; it is the one that says I, Me, et cetera, and dwells in the bones and the blood of the paternal kin.[43] The second (*ama*) is the immaterial double of each person, a double that has great magical powers, particularly to detect sorcerers that might attack the person and be responsible for his or her death. And the third soul (*kwela*) is associated with the flesh and the blood of the maternal clan. But the part that comes from these maternal kin is highly dangerous, and if an

---

42   We now have a remarkable study on Fore mortuary rites conducted by an international team of doctors, J. Whitfield, W. H. Pako, J. Collinge and M. P. Alpers: 'Metaphysical personhood and traditional South Fore mortuary rites' (unpublished manuscript). See Whitfield et al., 'Mortuary rites of the South Fore and Kuru', *Philosophical Transactions of the Royal Society of London* (series B, Biological Sciences) 363 (2008), 3721–3724.

43   Whitfield et al. define souls as 'part or parts of the person that depart from the body at death'.

individual is to become an ancestor after death and reach the land of the dead, his or her being must be rid of the maternal part and thereby become a totally 'patrilineal' being.

That is precisely what the women are doing when they eat, little by little, the body of the dead, and they do this, they say, 'out of love and respect'. Only postmenopausal women are allowed to do this, and they belong, when the corpse is that of a married man, to the deceased's mother's clan and to the clan of his wife. These women thus belong to clans allied with that of the deceased. The act of eating a corpse lasts several days, interrupted by several purification rites for the women. The mourning period goes on for months. The deceased, who has now become an ideal person and a full member of the patrilineal clan, sets out for Kwelanamandi, taking with him or her the souls of all the taros, sweet potatoes, and so on left at the site of the death. When they arrive, a great welcoming celebration is organised in honour of the deceased by their ancestors. Produced by Bagina, the earth, the deceased returns to the earth. The Fore example is only one of hundreds that confirm the hypothesis that birth is conceived as the conjunction of elements, and death as their disjunction. This conception also contains the idea that, through their mortuary rites, the living help the deceased reach the dwelling place of the dead, where they will become an ancestor; the idea that the dwelling place of the dead is more pleasant than that of the living, since the burdens of the living no longer exist there: illness, famine, war, sorcery; and the idea that humans are born from the earth by means of a magical act, by a creation, and that the earth itself has neither beginning nor end; and finally that all this is true because it is inscribed in the landscape, in the visible sacred places and in the words of the ancestors transmitted from one generation to the next. The mythic imaginary has thus turned into real social relations between men and women, initiates and noninitiates, consanguins and affines, into rites and rituals and therefore into ancestral institutions.[44] The mythic imaginary is conceived and experienced in these societies not as belonging to the

---

44   See also Godelier, *Lévi-Strauss*, 279–484.

realm of unreal reality, but as the most real form of reality, the basis of all reality, human and nonhuman, visible and invisible. The cosmological myths illuminate the rites and rituals; and the rituals continuously attest to the truth of the myths, of the words of the ancestors. We have here the circular proof typical of human thinking whenever it remains prisoner of its beliefs. As Geertz wrote concerning Bali: 'The world as lived and the world as imagined . . . turn out to be the same world.'[45]

Even if a Fore has committed crimes that remain unpunished in his lifetime, once he has died and become an ancestor, when he reaches Kwelananamandi, the land of the dead, he is supposed to enjoy the same afterlife as any other Fore. He will not be pursued by a postmortem judgment. This is clearly not the case in the religions of deliverance – Hinduism or Buddhism – or in those of salvation – Christianity and Islam. When a Hindu dies and is cremated, the soul appears before Yama, the god of death, who weighs the merits and demerits accumulated by the deceased in life. Depending on his judgment, the soul reenters the cycle of rebirths to be reincarnated in another existence or goes directly to the world of the gods, where it becomes an ancestor, while part is joined with Brahman, the universal principle. The transmigration of souls (samsara) ceases when the life debt is paid in full to the gods and deliverance achieved. In the monotheistic religions of salvation, after the person's death, the soul is judged by God, and depending on the gravity of the sins the person committed on earth during their lifetime, the soul is destined to spend eternity in hell or in heaven.[46] At the end of the twelfth century, the Christian imaginary created a third space in the afterlife: purgatory, a hell for a time but not forever, and ultimately the antechamber of paradise.[47]

The Christian imaginary thus went much further than that of the Fore. First of all, it affirmed that there is only one God, who created

45   C. Geertz, *The Interpretation of Cultures* (London: Hutchinson, 1973), 112.

46   Godelier, ed., *La mort et ses au-delà*, 9–50.

47   J. Le Goff, *The Birth of Purgatory* (Chicago: University of Chicago Press, 1986). See also Le Goff, ed., *Histoire et imaginaire* (Paris: Poiesis, 1986).

everything from nothing. Then, it declared that this single God is the union of three persons – Father, Son and Holy Spirit – and affirmed that Jesus of Nazareth, son of a humble carpenter, Joseph, and of Mary, was precisely the son of this God and therefore God himself. And finally, it proclaimed that the Son of God became a human being and was crucified to save humankind from its sins, and that he promised his followers eternal life in heaven at the right hand of God. Instead of the opposition between merits and demerits, as in Hinduism, here we have the opposition between righteousness and sin. Instead of humans helping the deceased to reach the dwelling place of the dead where they will lead a happy life, it is God who decides the fate of the deceased and who, depending on the number and the gravity of their breaches of the Ten Commandments, sentences them to eternal torture in hell or gathers them to himself in heaven.

The heart of the Christian mystery thus lies in the sacrifice of Christ, of a God who allowed himself to be tortured and put to death for the love of humanity and the 'redemption' of its sins. This sacrifice is reproduced each time a Catholic or Orthodox priest celebrates the mass. Indeed, when the priest consecrates the bread and the wine with his words, and gives them to the faithful in the sacrament of communion,[48] God himself intervenes to turn the bread and the wine into his body and his blood, which only appear to be bread and wine. This is the mystery of transubstantiation, that is to say, the belief in the real and nonsymbolic transformation of the bread and the wine into Christ's body and blood.[49] When this occurs, the words spoken by Jesus at the last supper with his disciples, as reported by Saint John, come true: 'Anyone who does eat my flesh and drink my blood has eternal life, and I shall raise him up on the last day. For my flesh is real

48   Orthodox Christians take communion in both kinds; before the second Vatican Council, Roman Catholics, with the exception of the priest, used to take only the bread.

49   For Calvin, the bread and the wine are merely symbols, metaphors, but already in the seventh century CE, Saint Macarius disputed this interpretation: 'This is not the symbol of the body or the symbol of the blood, as some blind minds have dressed it up, but well and truly the body and the blood of Christ.'

food and my blood is real drink. He who eats my flesh and drinks my blood lives in me and I live in him.'[50]

The idea of transubstantiation already existed in antiquity, before the word was invented to designate this mystery. We find it in Saint Ignatius (d. 107 CE), Saint Irenaeus (140–202 CE), Saint John Chrysostom (344–407 CE), and so on. The term itself appeared in 1079 CE with Hildebert of Tours, at the time of the Council of Rome. Transubstantiation was declared dogma in 1215 at the Fourth Lateran Council, organised to combat the Albigensian heresy, and was officially adopted at the Council of Trent (1545–1563):

> If any one shall deny, that, in the sacrament of the most holy Eucharist, are verily, *really*, and substantially contained the *body* and *blood*, together with the *soul* and divinity, of our Lord Jesus Christ, and consequently the whole Christ; but shall say that He is only therein as in a *sign*, or in *figure*, or virtue; let him be anathema.[51]

Here we find what we were saying about sacred or holy objects. They do not represent the divine; they presentify it. The bread and the wine are neither signs nor figures of Christ. To be sure, they are symbols for Christ when they *have not yet* been consecrated by the priest's words. But once these words have been pronounced, they are *more than* that. It is Christ as God who sacrificed himself on the cross who is entirely present in the species and with whom the faithful are going to be able to communicate, to incorporate into themselves.[52] As in the case of the boli made by a priest in the service of the Bambara king – who, through his prayers and rituals, made the god present in

---

50   Gospel of Saint John 6: 53–57. *The Jerusalem Bible* (Garden City, NY: Doubleday & Company).

51   *Canons and Decrees of the Council of Trent*, session 13, canon 1, trans. T. A. Buckley (London: George Routledge & Co., 1851); my emphasis.

52   After the consecration, the Roman Catholic liturgy used to add (in our English translation): 'May Your Body that I have eaten and Your Blood that I have drunk cleave to my entrails.' Cf. V. Zubizarreta, *Traité de théologie dogmatique*, vol. 4, Vittoria, 1948.

the object he had made with his hands, and who would help the king be victorious in war – the Catholic priest or the Orthodox pope, through the formula consecrating the bread and wine made by human hands, brings about the presence of Christ in person in the bread and the wine. The presence is 'real', because the bread and the wine no longer invoke an unreal, virtual presence, as in play or art, with the teddy bear or the *Mona Lisa*. They have become not only the container for a god, but the god himself, who, in offering himself to his faithful in communion, reproduces the sacrifice he made of his person by allowing himself to be crucified to redeem humankind from sin. In this, the Eucharist differs in two aspects from all other sacraments. It renders Christ bodily present, whereas the other sacraments contain only God's grace. Contrary to the other sacraments, it is a sacrifice through which believers communicate with their God, 'find themselves' in him, 'incorporate' him into themselves.

The religious imaginary thus effects a *veritable mutation in the nature of the symbols*. This is a fundamental point. Religious symbols are no longer merely material, cultural realities made by humans and chosen to signify the god (his body, blood and soul) and communicate with him. They are transformed by the divinity into a means *for him* to communicate with humans and act on them from within. It is no longer humans who, on their own, give meaning to their symbols; it is also the god who, through these symbols, speaks to them and acts on them by his presence and his actions. God or the gods add meaning to the symbols invented by humans in order to speak to them, a meaning that humans could not have invented by themselves, a meaning they receive. However, in order to follow this meaning that emanates from God or the gods, we must believe in it. And to believe, in this case, is to believe the unbelievable; not to believe in what we see, but in what we do not see; to set aside the doubts that experience and/or reason can raise. To believe is to have absolute trust in what is said; it is to have 'faith'.

Saint Thomas Aquinas offers proof of this. This thirteenth-century saint is the author of the office of the feast known as the Feast of the Holy Sacrament or of the 'Body of Christ', which had just been established. In his *Summa Theologica*, he develops a 'rational' explanation of the mystery of the transubstantiation and the 'real' presence of Christ's body in the bread and the wine, basing his argument on Aristotle. The latter distinguished material bodies into their invisible substance and their accidents, their perceptible qualities. Saint Thomas defines transubstantiation as the conversion, through the action of God, of the whole substance of the bread into Christ's body, and the whole substance of the wine into Christ's blood, with the exception of the appearances of the bread and the wine, which remain as they were before the consecration.[53] The conversion is real, then, but invisible. This explanation was obviously not meant for the millions of faithful who lived in the countrysides and towns of Christian Europe at the time, but for the elite, who read Latin and were capable of understanding concepts borrowed from an Ancient Greek philosopher. For the masses of believers, Saint Thomas appealed simply to their faith:

> The presence of Christ's true body and blood in this sacrament cannot be detected by sense, nor understanding, but by faith alone, which rests upon Divine authority . . . This argument holds good of Christ's bodily presence, as He is present after the manner of a body, that is as it is in its visible appearance, but not as it is spiritually, that is, invisible, after the manner and by the virtue of the spirit.[54]

To believe is therefore to presume the unbelievable to be true, to trust that the impossible is possible. Saint Ambrose (ca. 340–397) already put it well when he wrote of the (magical) power of the blessing of the bread and the wine: 'Christ's words were able to create what was not; could they not therefore change what is into what was not? This body that we make present is the body born of the Virgin. Why

---

53   Saint Thomas Aquinas, *Summa Theologica*, III 9, 76, a.7: Christ's body is substantially present in this sacrament. But substance, as such, is not visible to the physical eye, nor does it come under any one of the senses or under the imagination, but solely under the intellect, whose object is 'what a thing is'.

54   Ibid., III 9, 75, a.1.

seek, here, in Christ's body, the order of Nature, whereas the Lord
Jesus himself was born of the Virgin Mary, *outside of Nature's laws*.[55]

To believe is thus to presume the truth of the affirmations of the
existence of facts that are not of 'the natural order',[56] and therefore of
supernatural facts that attest the existence of another reality, an invisible reality that is even more real than the visible real, since it is its
(metaphysical) foundation. To believe is to know we have access to
the 'real' meaning of the things of life. Pascal recognised as much
when he wrote: 'When the word of God, which is really true, is false
literally, it is true spiritually.'[57]

The problem raised here is a fundamental one: Why does that
which is true as a truth higher than any other for those who believe
the dogmas of a religion appear to be totally imaginary for those who
do not believe? For Muhammad and Muslims, Jesus is not the son of
God nor God himself; he is the last of the Jewish prophets who came
before Muhammad, who saw himself as the true spokesman of Allah,
the one and only God. It is as though the imaginary content of religions was obvious only from the *outside*, for followers of another religion or of none. That is why the symbols of a given religion – crucifix,
bread, wine, ritual formulas, liturgical gestures – are 'objects' that 'say'
nothing 'sacred' to the billions of non-Christians. But for Christians,
these symbols are loaded with meaning and have all the more effect
on them and in them because they evoke the most real of realities,
even though these exist beyond the rational sphere. Lamblicus (d. 325
CE) noted that 'the unexplained power of the symbol gives us access
to the things of God'.[58] Loaded with meanings men did not put there,
religious symbols therefore oblige those who handle them to discover

---

55   Our emphasis.

56   Such as creating the world from nothing, the Immaculate Conception of the
Virgin Mary, Jesus's resurrection and his ascension into heaven, etc.

57   B. Pascal, *Pensées* (Paris: Flammarion, 1976), 687.

58   P. Sbalchiero, *Dictionnaire des miracles et de l'extraordinaire chrétien* (Paris:
Fayard, 2002), 775. Jung can be placed in this tradition since he defined the symbol as 'not
an arbitrary or intentional sign standing for a known and conceivable fact but an admittedly
anthropomorphic – hence a limited and partly valid – expression for something suprahu-
man and only partly conceivable' (*Psyche and Symbols* [New York: Doubleday, 1958], 152).

the sense delivered but always hidden. That is the purpose of all hermeneutical endeavours (the Kabbalah, Chinese hexagrams, etc.).

To conclude on the importance of believing and belief, we will follow Charles Malamoud, who takes us to the India of the Vedas. Belief in the gods is not considered to be simply a disposition of the mind – in Sanskrit, 'belief' is *sraddha*, also translated as 'trust' – rather, this disposition is divinised. To believe is to be in the power of the goddess Belief. 'It is she who causes the other gods to exist because it is she *who gives meaning to the rites* which, in turn, *gives the gods consistency*'.[59] In order for God to be, he must be believed. 'How then can the goddess Belief be made to believe within us?' She must be invoked by 'what is True', and this is none other than the Vedic texts: 'words of truth whose truth does not need to be proven or even believed'.[60] For Hindus, the Vedas were not written by human hand. They are words that the ancient sages (the *sri*) heard, transcribed and transmitted down to the present day. This is a wonderful demonstration of a recurring mechanism that produces the religious imaginary. The humans who invented the gods, and who are at the origin of the holy texts in which they believe, disappear from these beginnings; in their place, gods and spirits appear, who reveal to these humans the myths and rituals that will guide them in life; but this was invented by humans as well. By this inversion of cause and effect, something that belongs to humankind became detached and transformed into an invisible world, populated by more or less powerful entities that dominate humans and from whom humankind must ever after beg protection and blessings; and it is even more powerful when it comes to salvation – in other words, the forgiveness of sins committed by humans in the course of their lives – or when it comes to deliverance – the disappearance of suffering, undergone or inflicted, over their lifetime.

---

59 C. Malamoud, *Féminité de la parole. Études sur l'Inde Ancienne* (Paris: Albin Michel, 2005), 228.

60 Ibid., 232–233.

CHAPTER NINE

The Imaginary of Political-Religious Systems

We now turn to the imaginary and the symbolic present at the heart of power systems. State-based political systems, which appeared successively starting some 3,500 years BCE – Sumer, Ancient Egypt, the Shang Dynasty in China, among others – had a great variety of forms of sovereignty – city-states, kingdoms, empires – and all either fused or closely associated political and religious functions. This is because the exercise of power was included in a cosmic and religious view of nature and society, and because those who exercised power did so legitimately, having been chosen by the gods or being themselves descendants of the gods.

The Chinese emperor, the wang, was 'the unique man', who had received 'the Mandate of Heaven' to govern. He was the only human to have the right to celebrate the rituals designed to bring abundance to the peoples of the empire. In Egypt, the pharaoh, a god dwelling among humans, would sail his sacred boat up the Nile every year when the waters were at their lowest and, upon reaching the headwaters, would perform the rituals that begged the river god again next year to bring back the silt-laden waters that would flood the fields the peasants had laid out along its banks.

The Inca claimed to descend from Inti, the sun god, and partook of his divinity. Every year he would 'symbolically' clear the garden of the Coricancha, the great temple of the sun at Cuzco, where he would plant golden stalks of maize, whose leaves and ears were made of the precious metal. He would also plant golden specimens of other plants cultivated in his empire. By means of this ritual, the Inca, with the help of the sun god, was believed to ensure flourishing harvests and material well-being for all peoples and tribes of his empire. And if harvests were poor and famine threatened, the Inca, in his benevolent goodness, would order the state grain stores, filled with the tribute imposed by force on his subjects, to be opened and the contents distributed to the needy.[1] The mummies of the Inca's ancestors owned lands and herds whose product was destined for their worship. This cult was ensured by priests attached to the ancestors together with a labour force of men and women who had been drawn from the various peoples of the empire and had the status of yanacona.[2]

In the Maya kingdom, the kings of the different city-states were related to the god of maize, the staple of their populations, and they were supposed to join him when they died and be taken into him.[3] In Polynesia, the great chiefs and the nobles possessed something of the divinity in their bodies: mana. In Tonga, the tu'i tonga, the paramount chief, descended from Tangaloa, one of the greatest gods of the Polynesian pantheon. And in the eighteenth century, the great chiefs of the islands of Hawaii and Maui had become godlike kings, with whom Captain Cook's meeting, in 1778 and 1779, would lead to the latter's death.[4]

Political power mingled with religious power, in the persons of human beings who were close to the gods or descendants of gods, if not gods themselves, is one of the ways of legitimising the various forms of sovereignty exercised over humans and over the natural environment. Such a fusion of powers characterises the earliest appearances of the state in Sumer and in Egypt, as well as the first Chinese kingdoms that preceded the establishment of the empire. Furthermore, until the early twentieth century CE, forms of combined political and religious powers were found in the African kingdoms that had survived the colonial period and which have been the object of remarkable studies by British and French anthropologists. A

---

1   Of course, all such rites disappeared with the conquest of Peru by the Spanish, who destroyed the Inca Empire, killed its emperors and confiscated their lands, while the Catholic priests worked to 'stamp out idol worship' in the populations.

2   A. Métraux, *Les Incas* (Paris: Seuil, 1962), 97. The yanacona were men and women detached from their original community and attached to the service of the Inca nobility.

3   N. Grube, ed., *Mayas, una civilizacion milenaria* (Cologne: Könemann, 2000).

4   P. V. Kirch, *How Chiefs Became Kings: Divine Kingship and the Rise of Archaic States in Ancient Hawai'i* (Berkeley: University of California Press, 2010).

number of passages and phrases describing forms of royal power separated by several thousands of years attest to this.

To characterise the pharaoh's power, B. Menu, in her book *Maât. L'ordre juste du monde*,[5] defines the king in the following way: 'The King is of supernatural essence. He exists before his birth and after his death. He guarantees an order that is both cosmic and terrestrial, divine and human, general and particular, which would be called maât.'[6]

Maât is order, life; cosmic, social and vital balance; prosperity, justice, fairness and truth. Its antonym is *isfet*, meaning disorder, chaos, destitution, injustice, unfairness, lies. The notion already accompanied the establishment of Ancient Egypt's founding dynasty, that of King Narmer, who unified the kingdoms of Upper and Lower Egypt. The pharaoh is conceived as the son of Re, the sovereign god of the universe, and his mission is to maintain a state of maât, to keep isfet, disorder, enemies, hardship, and other perils at bay. A hymn from the Middle Empire celebrated the pharaoh in the following terms.

> Rê has set the king over the land of the living
> forever and all eternity
> so that he may judge mankind and satisfy the gods
> bring about Maat and annihilate Isfet
> He makes sacrifices to the gods
> and funerary offerings
> to the immortalised dead.[7]

Keystone of the cosmic and social order, the pharaoh sends out his life breath, *kha*, to all living creatures, human and nonhuman, so that every being owes its life to him. Humans in particular owe him absolute obedience and tribute of their labour force and their products.

---

5   B. Menu, *Maât: L'ordre juste du monde* (Paris: Michalon, 2005).
6   Ibid., 9; our translation.
7   Ibid., 23; our translation.

Therefore, a pharaoh is not a sort of supreme chief, a man reigning over men with the help of the gods; he is a god who reigns over men with the help of the gods and men.

Let us now go to Africa of the 1930s and 40s, where several anthropologists, led by Meyer Fortes and Evans-Pritchard, were studying the Ankole, Kede and Zulu, together with other groups, and the way they functioned. In 1940, they published their findings in a landmark book, *African Political Systems*,[8] prefaced by Radcliffe-Brown. The latter alerted the reader from the outset:

> In Africa it is often hardly possible to separate, even in thought, political office from ritual or religious office. Thus in some African societies it may be said that the king is the executive head, the legislator, the supreme judge, the commander-in-chief of the army, the chief priest or supreme ritual head, and even perhaps the principal capitalist of the whole community. But it is erroneous to think of him as combining in himself a number of separate and distinct offices. There is the single office, that of king, and its various duties and activities, and its rights, prerogatives, and privileges, make up a single unified whole.[9]

In France, too, beginning in the 1960s, anthropologists of West and Central Africa published a constellation of remarkable studies on various African kingdoms – Cameroon, Burkina Faso, Chad, the Congo, and others. For some of them, it seemed that the head of these kingdoms was more like a medium than a priest.[10]

---

8   M. Fortes and E. E. Evans-Pritchard, eds, *African Political Systems* (London: Oxford University Press, 1940), xxi.

9   Ibid.

10   Allow me to mention Georges Balandier's pioneering book *La Vie quotidienne au Royaume de Kongo du XVIe au XVIIIe siècles* (Paris: Hachette, 1965); and then an overview, *Anthropologie politique* (Paris: PUF, 1967); and É. Dampierre, *Un royaume bandia du Haut-Oubangui* (Paris: Plon, 1967). Then came A. Adler, *Le Pouvoir et l'interdit. Royauté et religion en Afrique noire* (Paris: Albin Michel, 2010); M. Augé, *Théorie des pouvoirs et idéologie* (Paris: Hermann, 1975); J. Bazin, 'Genèse de l'État et formation d'un champ politique: le royaume de Segu', *Revue française de science*

Another form of state power is the close association of political power and religious functions without their fusion in a single person. This was the case in the Ancient Greek city-states, but also in Rome under the Republic. Jupiter was the *primus civis*, the first among Roman citizens. The laws drawn up by magistrates and voted upon by the Senate were submitted to him for his approval, which the god always granted. The religious rituals were meant to ensure the *pax deorum*, and no Roman citizen had the right to abstain: 'Religion is only one face of a single reality that can be called City, Republic.'[11] For Jupiter is the chief god and, at the same time, the first among the citizens of the city of Rome. Roman men (but not women) were citizens and not subjects of 'great kings' such as Nebuchadnezzar or Darius.

Yet another combination of politics and religion grew up and developed in the Christian West with the disappearance of the Roman Empire and the fall of Rome. Alternatively, in Byzantium, in the Eastern Christian Empire, unlike in the 'Latin' West, the emperor was also a priest.[12] Indeed, the fall of Rome created a separation between Christianity and the city, which it was supposed to serve. As Jean-Philippe Genet writes, 'The Roman concept of "public religion" is evacuated [and] the Church appears, de facto, as the only guarantor of the sacred.' Furthermore, the Church provided the 'overall framework

politique 5, 709–719; M. Izard, *Gens de pouvoir, gens de la terre* (Paris: Éditions de la Maison des Sciences de l'Homme; Cambridge: Cambridge University Press, 1985); C. Tardits, *Le Royaume bamoum* (Paris: Armand Colin, 1980); E. Terray, *Une histoire du royaume abron du Gyaman* (Paris: Karthala, 1995). See also the comparison between various African forms of kinship and those in Europe, in E. Le Roy Ladurie, ed., *Les Monarchies*, symposium, Paris, 8–10 December 1981 (Paris: PUF, 1986). And finally, let me mention, as well, L. de Heusch, *Le Roi ivre ou l'origine de l'État* (Paris: Gallimard, 1972).

11   J. Scheid, *Religion et piété à Rome* (Paris: La Découverte, 1985; Seuil, 2001), 174; and especially, Scheid, *Les Dieux, l'État et l'individu* (Paris: Seuil, 2013). 'Only the civic community, the *res publica*, of the Roman people was endowed with a religious personality, and its endowment was collective', 157; our translation.

12   G. Dagron, *Empereur et prêtre. Étude sur le 'ecésaro-papismee' byzantin* (Paris: Gallimard, 1996). See A. Boureau, 'Des politiques tirées de l'Écriture. Byzance et l'Occident', *Annales HSS* (2000), 879–887.

of social and political life' and, in this sense, in the West, it was the successor to the empire.[13]

The pope represents the mystic union of the Church with Christ. He stands above the king, as, while kings are 'anointed',[14] that does not make them either priests or bishops. The coronation of the emperor by the pope, or of kings by bishops, certifies the legitimacy of their power in the Church's eyes. Confronted with the problem of the status of royal power, the Church fathers founded its legitimacy on the words of Saint Paul in his Letter to the Romans: 'You must all obey the governing authorities. Since all government comes from God, the civil authorities were appointed by God.'[15]

Furthermore, in the thirteenth century, when a king was crowned at Reims, he swore to keep the following three promises: 'First that the Christian people of the Church of God will keep the true peace under our administration. Secondly, that I will forbid pillaging and all forms of iniquity. Third, that in all my judgments, I will prescribe equity and mercy.'[16]

While they were anointed without thereby becoming priests authorised to celebrate the sacraments, kings could become saints and work miracles, like Louis IX (Saint Louis 1226–1270), who, upon returning from his expedition to Jerusalem, found himself able to cure those who came to him suffering from scrofulous.[17] All this is

13   J. P. Genet, 'Légitimation religieuse et pouvoir dans l'Europe médiévale latine', 393; our translation.

14   Cf. A. Lemaire, *Prophètes et rois* (Paris: Cerf, 2001). In ancient Israel, anointing was the sign that God, Yahweh, had chosen the person to become king. *Christos* means 'anointed'. Beginning in the eleventh century, the kings of France were crowned at Reims and anointed with Holy Chrism, an oil contained in the Holy Ampulla, which the Holy Spirit was supposed to have given the bishops of Reims.

15   Saint Paul's Letter to the Romans, 13: 1–4.

16   J. Le Goff et al., *Le sacre royal à l'époque de saint Louis d'après le manuscrit latin 1246 de la BnF* (Paris: Gallimard, 2001), 47–48. In the time of the Frankish kings, the king was first acclaimed by the freemen, and then anointed. The choice of the king by popular acclamation disappeared in the centuries that followed.

17   Cf. M. Bloch's pioneering work *The Royal Touch: Monarchy and Miracles in France and England* (Dorchester: Dorset Press, 1990 [1924]). For more on the subject of royal miracles, see J. Le Goff, 'La Genèse du miracle royal', in H. Atsma and A. Burguière, eds, *Marc Bloch aujourd'hui. Histoire comparée et sciences sociales* (Paris: EHESS, 1990), 147–156.

sufficient proof that the intertwining of the Christian religion and the exercise of power by the emperors or the kings of Christian Europe, together with the principle of subordinating the political sphere to that of religion, of kings to the Church or the pope, rested for centuries on the combination of imaginary elements having to do with belief and faith (the religious basis of the power of the popes and kings) with symbolic elements (coronation, anointment, the royal touch, etc.). To these two elements must be added the power of real violence (military, social, psychological – such as the Inquisition or the Saint Bartholomew's Day massacre) to silence or physically eliminate opponents. But at the same time, over the centuries, the kings of the various European countries tended to distance themselves from papal power or to reject it altogether (as was the case in England, and still is in Protestant Europe). In the seventeenth century, Louis XIV in France and Charles XI in Sweden[18] both declared themselves 'absolute' monarchs, although they exercised their absolute power differently when it came to religion and to their people.[19]

In short, until the French Revolution proclaimed that sovereignty lay with the people alone, who decided the laws to be applied to themselves, all forms of political sovereignty were either based on or legitimised with reference to the existence of gods or God. And in each case, these references to imaginary realities were embodied in real social institutions and symbolic practices whose presence confirmed the obvious truth of these founding myths. Religion did not cease to exist with the separation of the political and religious spheres which spread over Europe in the twentieth century, but it has now become a private or community affair. This is a striking social and mental

---

18   A. Upton, *Charles XI and Swedish Absolutism* (Cambridge: Cambridge University Press, 1998).

19   It should be remembered – for the fact sends a strong signal – that, after the French Revolution, which abolished the monarchy in France and declared the republic defended by General Bonaparte, when, on 2 December 1804, the latter wanted to have himself crowned emperor in the church of Notre Dame in Paris, he personally crowned himself with a gold crown of laurel leaves, after the custom of the Roman emperors, which was a copy of Charlemagne's crown. See Genet, 'Légitimation religieuse et pouvoir dans l'Europe médiévale latine', 383.

transformation within these societies, even if the principle of secularism (*laïcité* in French)[20] continues to be a hotly debated issue. For Islam, since the only recognised sovereignty is that of God, and since all human law is based on the sharia, the God-given law that is to be respected even before it is interpreted, kings and heads of state are bound to govern in accordance with the Koran.[21]

So as not to leave the reader with the (false) impression that the fusion or the close association of religion with the exercise of power is found only in societies where sovereignty over a territory, its resources and its inhabitants is exercised by some form of state, and therefore by those controlling and governing their society, I will cite here the account of the foundation of the Baruya society.

The Baruya are a tribe in Papua New Guinea with whom I lived and worked for many years. They were unfamiliar with the state before being suddenly and violently subjected to the power of the Australian colonial state in 1960. Until that time, the Baruya had governed themselves without a state, and their society was not divided into orders, or castes, or classes, but into clans. In short, for Westerners, they were 'real primitives' who needed to be civilised and Christianised (colonisation + Christianisation = civilisation).

The Baruya belong to the group of non-Austronesian peoples, the oldest inhabitants of Papua New Guinea, whose arrival on the island preceded that of Austronesian-speaking groups by some 10,000 years. Some of the latter, after having left South China and Taiwan around 3000 BCE, set out to conquer the Pacific, living for a time on the coasts of the islands where they landed and finally, during the first millennium of our era, becoming the ancestors of those known as 'Polynesians', after having settled in the heart of the South Pacific in a

---

20   *Laïcité* has particular overtones in French and is the subject of public debate. The French word signifies the total separation between the political, as the power exercised by the state, and the religious, i.e., all religions. The state allows all citizens to practice their religion, if they have one, or not to practise any religion. France has no state religion.

21   B. Lewis, *Le langage politique de l'Islam* (Paris: Gallimard, 1988). Kings are humans who have not been chosen by God but by men, unlike the caliph, therefore, who heads the Umma, the Islamic community of believers.

vast zone bordered by Fiji, Samoa and Tonga. But the Baruya knew nothing of this.

However, they did know that they had not always lived in the mountains where they do now, but in Bravegareubaramandeuc, in a valley several days away on foot. They knew that at that time they belonged to another tribe, the Yoyue, but that they had been forced to flee their villages following the massacre of some of their numbers by the Tapache, an enemy tribe the other Yoyue clans had recruited to commit this massacre. The fugitives had taken refuge in the Marawaka Valley, among the Andje, one of whose clans, the Ndelie, had allowed them to hunt on and cultivate part of their territory. Some generations later, after having exchanged women with the Ndelie and adopted their language (which was very close to their own), the Baruya joined them in a plot to set a trap for the other Andje clans. They massacred a number of them, and the rest fled, abandoning their lands, which the victors appropriated. A new tribe was born when the victors initiated their boys in a shared ceremony, performing the rituals in the *tsimia*, the big house built for this purpose and which the Baruya call the 'body' of their tribe, each post being set in the ground by the father of an initiate. The new tribe took the name of the clan, Baruya, that owned the sacred objects, the *kwaimatnie*, the most important of which – with the help of the Sun and the Moon, two gods worshipped by the Baruya – enabled them to make boys into warriors, shamans, et cetera. This was done through the male and female initiations, which involved all boys and all girls, regardless of clan, lineage or home village.

Initiations thus bring the tribe into existence as a whole and at the same time legitimise the men's (but not the women's) right to exercise power in their society, to govern it and to represent it to neighbouring (friendly or hostile) tribes. In enabling the society to exist and be represented as a whole, the initiations ensure a function equivalent to that of the state in a society divided into orders, castes or classes. Constructing the big ceremonial house, the tsimia; initiating the boys in order to make them into warriors who will defend the tribe's territory; initiating the girls so they will be fertile and conceive children for the lineage of their husband, whom they must obey, are acts that found a tribal society. This foundation is repeated each time the Baruya men initiate a new generation of boys and the Baruya women a new generation of girls.

To sum up: for the Baruya, founding their society meant constructing a tsimia for the first time and performing the rituals there. Subsequently, each time an initiation is held, the village fires are extinguished, and a new fire is lit by striking sacred flint stones together, whose sparks will ignite a handful of fibres and twigs. The clan responsible for kindling the new fire is the Andavakia, the clan to which the tribe's most important shaman has belonged for generations. I believe I have given readers enough historical and sociological information to allow them to discover, in the following story of how the initiations came about, the inextricable intertwining of a mythic account and historical events.[22]

In olden times all people lived in one place, a place located near a big water [the sea?].[23] One day the people separated and our own ancestor, the Kwarrandariar, the Kwarrandariar-Baruya, the Kwarrandariar lineage of the Baruya clan rose up into the air and flew to the spot where we lived afterwards, Bravegareubaramandeuc, not far from Menyamya. The name of our ancestor was Djivaamakwe, and Djivaamakwe flew in the air along a fiery red path. This path was like a bridge that the *wandjinia* [men of the dreamtime, those who lived in the beginning] had built for Djivaamakwe and for the *kwaimatnie* that Sun had given our ancestor before he flew away. Sun is the man

---

22   For more on initiation rites and the makeup of the Baruya society, see M. Godelier, *The Making of Great Men: Male Domination and Power among the New Guinea Baruya*, trans. R. Swyer (Cambridge: Cambridge University Press, 1986). For accounts of the foundation of Ancient Greek city-states, see J. Scheid and J. Svenbro, *La tortue et la lyre. Dans l'atelier du mythe antique* (Paris: CNRS, 2014).

23   The Baruya language has no word for the sea, because they did not know of its existence. But the expression 'big water' in the myth may allude to a remote time when the ancestors of the Baruya and of other tribes lived by the sea and were later driven into the country's interior highlands by Austronesian groups that, in the course of their migration, settled for a few generations on the shores of Papua New Guinea.

in the middle. He sees everything and everyone at the same time. Djivaamakwe received three kwaimatnie, three *mukamaye*.[24] When he touched the ground, the wandjinia revealed to him the name, Kanaamakwe, the secret name of the Sun.[25] They also revealed to him the name of the place and the name he must give to the men he would find there: the Baragaye. Baruya is the name of an insect with red wings with black spots, which the members of the Baruya clan must not kill. Its wings are like the red path that took Djivaamakwe to Bravegareubaramandeuc.

There were men there. He gave them their (clan) names, Andavakia, Nunguye, Bakia, et cetera. Then he set up the male initiations. He explained that a boy had to become *muka*, then *palittamunie*, then *chuwanie* and so forth.[26] And he gave them all ritual tasks to perform and had them build a tsimia. Then he told them: 'I am the centre post of this house, the tsimaye.[27] You are under me. I am the first, and the first name all of you will have will be mine, Baruya.' The others, the Andavakia, the Nunguye, et cetera, did not object when he raised his own name, the name of the Baruya-Kwarrandariar, and lowered their names, the Andavakia, Nunguye, et cetera. They had little kwaimatnie. He said that he was tsimaye, the centre post, and the others said to him: 'Your two names are Baruya-Tsimia'. He said to them: 'Now try out your kwaimatnie. Try them out doing what I told you to do in the initiations.' And they said to him: 'We are your warriors'. We cannot let you get killed by enemies. You will not go to war. We will go and you will stay among us.' This was because, from

---

24   *Muka* designates the first-stage initiates who have just had their nose pierced; *maye* means flower.

25   Women are not supposed to know this name.

26   These are the names of the first three initiation stages, of which there are four in all. The boys are separated from the world of their mothers and of women in general around the age of nine, and will leave the men's house when they are around twenty to marry a girl their clan has chosen for them.

27   The *tsimaye* is also called 'grandfather' or 'ancestor'. At the top of this huge pole, the Bakya clan plants four long sticks, called *nilamaye* (flowers: *maye*; *nila*: sun) designed to call the sun closer to the tsimia and to the men who are going to initiate the boys and the young men.

the moment Djivaamakwe came down at Bravegareubaramandeuc, there were many wars and wars 'for nothing'. It is because of the ceaseless warring that Yaruemeie, Djivaamakwe's son, had to flee from Bravegareubaramandeuc and take refuge in Maruaka.[28] But he had taken the kwaimatnie, the Sun's gift, with him. In Maruaka, our ancestors changed their name. The Ndelie took them in and allowed them to live at Kwarrandariar. Ever since we have been the Baruya-Kwarrandariar. Then the Ndelie helped us conquer the Andje and take over their territory and, to thank them, our ancestor at the time, whose name was also Djivaamakwe, the other's grandson, gave the Ndelie the third kwamatnie given by the Sun and roles in the initiations. That is why we only have two now. And Djivaamakwe, in front of the beaten enemies, in front of the Anjde, dressed the young men and set their insignia on their heads. Then he said 'these here will be *aoulatta* (great warriors), these here will be *kulaka* (shamans)', et cetera. He saw and marked those who would become *apmwenangalo* (great men).

For someone who is not a Baruya, this story appears to be basically a myth legitimising the status of the Baruya clan – and particularly the Kwarrandariar lineage – as the centre post of the tribe, a status with which they were vested by the Sun. They say of the Sun that he is their father (*numwe*) and that they are all children of the Sun. This is more than just a metaphor because, before their conversion to Christianity, the Baruya believed a child was conceived conjointly by the Sun and a man. The man's semen made only the foetus, which did not have a nose, fingers or toes. Each time, it was the Sun who completed the foetus in the woman's womb and gave it a human shape. The woman did not engender the child then. Her uterus was referred to as a *gilia*, the same word used for the netbags the women make to carry their loads of taros, sweet potatoes and other produce from the gardens

---

28   After this sentence, the story refers to events that are historical, but which have been made into legends. Intertribal warfare in Papua New Guinea was endemic, hence the expression 'warriors for nothing'. But to be recognised as a 'great warrior' one must go to war, kill enemies and multiply the pretexts for this.

they cultivate, and above all on top of which they perch their last-born, comfortably nestled in its own little netbag.

As the account shows, in such a warlike society as the Baruya, the fact that certain clans owned sacred objects and formulae that magically implemented powers raised these clans above the others because they were closer to the Sun than the others and had been chosen to make their society and enable it to survive, and to conquer their enemies. This (relative) hierarchy among the clans that made up their society was based on what we in the West call political-religious powers.

The above was told us in 1979 by Yaruemeie, at the time a young man, who, following the unexpected death of his uncle Ypmeye, a man of prestige and authority, had just inherited responsibility for the rites of passage in the second and third stages of the initiations. This ritual is very important because the third stage, *tchuwanie*, corresponds to the generation of young men between the ages of fifteen and eighteen, who have reached puberty and can now go to war alongside the adults. At the same time, their lineage is preparing to find a wife for them by exchanging a – real or classificatory – sister for a girl from another lineage. The boys are not told of these negotiations and their outcome until the future wife menstruates for the first time and goes through the female initiations. Let me add that, among the clans who possess kwaimatnie and intervene at some point in the initiations, only the representative of the Kwarrandariar lineage has the right to place on the young tchuwanie's head and to remove from it the beak of the great hornbill, symbol of the penis, and the circle of wild pig's teeth, symbol of the vagina, which confirm the boys' status as men superior to women and as warriors. Their own father may not do this – proof, if need be, that the initiations as a social order stand above that of kinship. This order is that of the unity of the tribe as a whole, of male domination and of the tie all have with the gods Sun and Moon, the spirits of the mountains and the rivers, and those of the ancestors. The cooperation of all clans possessing kwaimatnie is necessary, and not only the ritual work of the representative of the Baruya clan, so that all the boys of the tribe, whatever their clan, become men capable of daily reproducing their society and defending it against enemy attacks.

I must add something that shows the limits of male domination among the Baruya, though. All kwaimatnie exist in pairs and work as couples: one is male and the other female, and the more powerful of the two is always the woman kwaimatnie. It is the 'hottest', in other words the one with the most efficient magic, and only the custodian of the kwaimatnie for his clan may handle it. The other one, the male kwaimatnie, is left to his brothers and other men from his lineage who help him in his ritual functions and repeat after him the magical gestures he performs on the initiates' bodies.

The kwaimatnies' power is thus composed of the Sun's presence in the object, but also of the addition of the male and female powers. However, for the Baruya, this addition is possible only because in the beginning, men had managed to appropriate the women's powers and add them, bind them to those of the men. Meanwhile, the Baruya know that women have not been definitively disjoined from their powers, and that without the violence exercised on them and without the initiation of the boys far from their mothers and the female world, the women's powers would return into their bodies, and it would then be they who dominate the men. For the women had originally invented bows and arrows, in short, what we would call culture. The men, by stealing the sacred flutes played by the women, which enabled them to have children, deprived them of this power. Their uterus is now merely a netbag in which the man deposits his semen and conceives children, with the help of Sun. Today women no longer have the right to touch the bows or to make them. This myth thus reveals the deep ideological and cosmological underpinnings of the Baruya society.

For the sake of comparison, here is a second founding myth, historically more important than that of the Baruya. This is the story of the founding of the city of México-Tenochtitlan, which was to become the capital of the future Aztec empire. Here, too, at various points in the story, the myth mixes in historical events. Today we know that, in the twelfth century CE, groups of hunters and warriors, known as Chichimeca – in Nahuatl the equivalent of 'Barbarians' for the Ancient Greeks and Romans – roamed the arid lands of northern Mexico and began to migrate southward in successive waves, until they gradually came to occupy the central plateau.[29]

Among these, guided and driven by their god Uitzilopochtli through the voice of his 'god bearer' priests, a group of tribes, the Mexica, left Aztlán, their mythic dwelling place – hence the name Azteca, by which they were also known – and began their long march south. Attacked and driven back by enemy tribes, and betrayed by friendly groups, they finally arrived in 1325 in Central Mexico, where there were already established cities, which refused to yield a square foot of land and only tolerated the Mexica's settlement in the swamps in the middle of Lake Texcoco. They were thus in search of a more welcoming place when, one night, their god Uitzilopochtli called the priest, Quauhcoatl, and said to him: 'Go back among the reeds; there you will see the cactus Tenochtli and joyfully perched on it, stands the eagle, who devours and warms itself in the sun ... there will be your city Mexico-Tenochtitlan and great things will be done there.'[30] Quauhcoatl called the tribes together and harangued them: 'Let us go into the rushes and into the reeds, into the thick of this lake, and let us look where the Tunal (the prickly pear) grows, for our god said it and you cannot doubt it since everything he has announced to us has come true.' All bowed down and plunged into the reeds and rushes, and they were not long in discovering the vision they were seeking: 'In the rushes, in the reeds, stood the cactus Tenochtli, and on top, was the eagle – and when it saw the Mexica, it bowed its head . . . and their god said to them: "O Mexicans, this is the place." Then they wept, crying out: "Finally we have been worthy, we are rewarded, we have marvelled at the sign: here we will build our city." '[31]

---

29   J. Soustelle, *La vie quotidienne des Aztèques* (Paris: Hachette, 1955), 14; and Soustelle, *L'Univers des Aztèques* (Paris: Hermann, 1979), chap. 2.

30   C. Duverger, *L'Origine des Aztèques* (Paris: Seuil 1983), 102–103.

31   *Crónica Mexicayotl*, 62–66.

Moses was not the only prophet, then, to whom a god had promised a land. And the eagle perched on a cactus and devouring a serpent is today the symbol of the Republic of Mexico, featured on its flag.[32]

If, for a moment, we close our eyes to the violence entailed in the formation and expansion of states and empires and their rivalry; to the reduction to slavery, serfdom or other forms of individual or collective bondage or submission of populations; if we forget the villages razed, the temples burned, the gods taken away to be added to the victors' pantheon or desecrated; what else do we see? That before they were destroyed, subjected or disappeared, hundreds of societies living and thinking in similar or different manners had made their appearance and engaged on the path that led to cities and states, or which subjected them to the influence of the great religions; these societies had built on their own territory temples, palaces, fortresses for gods and for a portion of humankind – nobles, warriors, priests, et cetera – who were 'above' the rest of the population. They had also invented numerous signs of distinction, clothing, jewellery, ways of speaking and eating, and so forth to indicate the unequal status of the groups that composed these societies.

In this event, we can no longer speak as Lévi-Strauss did, in talking about myths, of three 'separate' levels found in both myths and societies: the real, the imaginary and the symbolic.[33] We now see that the imaginary, which is the basis of religions and present in political systems, is transformed each time into *real* social relations, into words, gestures, institutions, rituals, monuments and works of art that testify materially, symbolically and socially to the truth and efficacy of what, in each of these societies, the mind presumes to be true and legitimate.[34] Religious explanations of the world and of

---

32   For more on the importance of foundation stories and the analysis of their mythic and historical components, see M. Détienne, ed., *Tracés de fondation* (Leuven: Peeters; Paris: Editions de l'EPHE, 1990).

33   Lévi-Strauss, *The Origin of Table Manners*, 84; *The Naked Man*, 666.

34   One example among others is the creation of the city of Nkamba in Congo-Kinshasa by the descendants of Simon Kimbangu, who was born in 1887, arrested by the Belgians in 1921 and died in prison in 1951. Kimbangu thought Adam was black, and he predicted the end of white domination. His disciples proclaimed Nkamba the New Jerusalem,

humans' role in it become mental *armatures* and ideological *legitimisations* of the existence of real relations established between orders (Rome), castes (India) and classes (medieval Europe). Here is not the place to define or criticise these sociological concepts. But in each case, a fraction of humankind has imagined and created new social relations, new ways of thinking, acting and feeling, and has incorporated them into bodies, words and objects. And in each case, a fraction of humankind has folded in on itself in such a way as to reproduce more or less identically what it had imagined. A society remains prisoner of itself for as long as no internal transformations or external interventions cast doubt on or call into question its certitudes, in other words, what it sees as central to its survival.

The political-religious imaginary, therefore, is not opposed to the real as the imaginary of play is opposed to the course of ordinary life or to the imaginary of the artist of the *Mona Lisa*, whose portrait also suspends the course of life for those contemplating her. This is because when they are transformed into social relations – institutions, monuments, works of art or the raison d'être of social groups with different functions and statuses – the imaginary of religions and systems of power engender quite simply the framework of people's daily life in society. Art is part and parcel of the process of production and reproduction of these relations that encompass the life of every person and define their place in this shared, all-inclusive framework. But art is not the underlying source that invents these relations as it serves them. It renders them present and socially efficient in accordance with the materials, techniques and symbols it uses. Art can also sometimes anticipate the emergence of new relations, as in Orwell's novels and in science fiction more generally.

A question arises at this point: If different religions follow over the history of humankind, whether or not many disappear or no longer concern more than a few people; if all tribal religions consider that the religions of the other tribes may perhaps be as true as their

---

and their religion became the third official religion of Congo-Kinshasa. Cf. A. Melice, 'La Cité de Nkamba du Congo-Kinshasa. Kimbanguisme et son espace symbolique aujourd'hui' (unpublished manuscript). Today, others in Syria and Iraq founded a caliphate, as in the eighth century, in the name of Muhammad and the Koran.

own without being troubled by it; and if, on the contrary, religions aspiring to universality consider that all other religions are false; to what do we owe the permanence of 'religion' over the course of history, its rebirth in ever-new and modern forms (in the sense that they adapt to their time, for instance, Protestantism's break with traditionally dominant Catholicism).[35]

The answer is clear: religions provide humans with *global* answers to existentially fundamental questions that arise in all societies and in all periods. These questions are linked, and they intersect at numerous points when we attempt to answer them; hence the 'logical' character of theological and mythological systems. For example:

- What does it mean to be born, to live, to die?
- What is a man?
- What is a woman?
- What relations should we have with the invisible, with the ancestors, with the spirits, with the gods or God?
- What are plants, animals, the natural environment?
- Which humans have the right to exercise power over others, and why?

All these existential questions can be summed up in the three questions at the bottom of a famous painting by Gauguin: 'Where do we come from? What are we? Where are we going?'

All religions attempt to answer these three questions. Whereas their answers are largely imaginary, and always counterintuitive; and they are not only elements of a 'theoretical' discourse; they serve to *act*: to act on nature, on others, on ourselves; to act with the ancestors, with (or against) the spirits, and with (and on) the gods. What matters most for the majority of men and women who are neither shamans, nor priests, nor theologians nor philosophers, is to know what they must do in daily life, in accordance with the truths of their beliefs, to

---

35   Cf. M. Weber, *The Protestant Ethic and the Spirit of Capitalism*, trans. Talcott Parsons (London and New York: Routledge, 2001 [1930]).

deal with the basic problems life throws at them. This explains the importance of collective and individual rituals, and the obligation to observe them, even if, inwardly, one does not – or does no longer – subscribe.[36]

Unlike myths and religions, which explain everything in a few oral tales or in thousands of scholarly pages, modern sciences, whether experimental or deductive, do not explain everything. And each time they resolve one problem and bring us a better understanding of certain environmental mechanisms, or those going on in our body or our mind, other problems arise that must be addressed. The progress of knowledge is endless. Religions, on the other hand, offer wholesale explanations of the world, which found rules of conduct, a moral system; this is something science cannot do with as much ambition or force of conviction. Science can explain what is bad for people's health, demonstrate the existence of global warming and warn of the serious consequences if we do not do something. But these answers are never enough, given the immediate existential problems engendered by poverty, social inequality, wars and population transfers; but also by the death of a loved one, an incurable illness, and so on.

In short, scientific reasoning (but philosophical reasoning, too) is not contagious, whereas universal or national religions are. My analysis of the different types of imaginary springing from the continuous possibility of being at once absent in the present through the mind while being present through consciousness (which is also mind) in everyday life, or those which spring from play or the arts, or finally, the imaginary central to religions, clearly shows the error and illusion of Kant and the Enlightenment philosophers who boasted of confining religion exclusively 'within the boundaries of mere Reason'.[37]

---

36   As J. Shield showed so well for religion in Rome, a religion from which no citizen could opt out. J. Shield, *Quand faire c'est croire* (Paris: Aubier, 2005).

37   I. Kant, *Religion within the Boundaries of Mere Reason*, trans. and edited A. Wood, G. Di Giovanni (Cambridge: Cambridge University Press, 1998); and Hegel's violent criticism of him in his *Science of Logic*, ed. and trans. G. Di Giovanni (Cambridge: Cambridge University Press, 2010) for having 'driven him to renounce speculative thinking' (vol. 1., chap. 1). We find the same accusation in his *Faith and Knowledge*, trans. W. Cerf and H. S. Harris (Albany: SUNY Press, 1977).

There is no such thing as a religion whose theses and dogmas might be demonstrated by mere reason, made wholly convincing and acceptable because they are 'rational'. It follows that any attempt to 'stamp out' religion, all religions, from the life of humankind makes no sense, and in any event is impossible. What *is* possible is to disjoin, when they are joined or fused, the exercise of the political and that of religion, and to allow individuals to exercise their sovereignty together, whatever their religion or lack of one.

For the 'political' sphere, underpinned or not by religious beliefs and institutions, fulfils a specific function, as we have seen. It seeks to provide and often to impose answers to the most immediate existential problems, ones that are less abstract than knowing where we come from, what we are or where we are going. The political establishes and legitimises norms, for example, for access to land, control of a territory, legitimate use of force in society or between societies, and so forth. The political is therefore directly connected with the issues that daily shape the social and material life of the individuals and groups that make up a society. And bracketed by the religious and the political are all the other social inequalities or differences – between men and women, adults and the elderly or children. The political sphere cannot disappear, no more than religion can. It can exist without the existence of a state (e.g., acephalous tribal societies or chiefdoms) or through a form of state. This state can be despotic or democratic, and so on. But nowhere can political power exist without imaginary dimensions and contents. The motto 'Liberty, equality, fraternity' is loaded with such dimensions, but it is presented more as a work in progress than as a triumphant system set in stone.

THE CONDITIONS IN WHICH THE FIRST FORMS
OF STATE APPEARED: SOME HYPOTHESES

These different examples of forms of political power fused or closely associated with a religion will perhaps allow us to shed some light on certain conditions required for the appearance of the first forms of state, beginning in the fourth millennium BCE, at Sumer and in

Egypt, probably in the third millennium in North China and at the end of the second millennium in South America and Mesoamerica.[38] All suppose belief in the existence of a hierarchy of gods, and therefore in some form of polytheistic religion. All imply that power be exercised by what we call a king, whether this king is, as in Egypt, a god living among humans, the pharaoh, or as in Sumer, a *lugal*, a 'great man', close to the gods and allied with one of them before whom he stands in worshipful humility.[39] There is thus already a contrast and an opposition between these two forms of kingship; but each contains, in its essence and its exercise, a core of inextricably intertwined imaginary representations and symbolic practices that give it a social existence.

Let us read what Henri Frankfort wrote in a landmark book, *Kingship and the Gods*[40]:

The ancient Near East considered kingship the very basis of civilization. Only savages could live without a king. Security, peace and justice could not reign without a ruler to champion them . . . But if we refer to kingship as a political institution, we assume a point of view which would have been incomprehensible to the ancients. We imply that human policy can be considered by itself. The ancients, however, experienced human life as part of a widely spreading network of connections which reached beyond the local and the national communities into the hidden depths of nature and the powers that rule nature. The purely secular – in so far as it could be granted to exist at all – was the purely trivial. Whatever was

---

38   J. L. Huot, *Une archéologie des peuples du Proche Orient* (Paris: Errance, 2004); B. Midant-Reynes, *Aux origines de l'Égypte. Du néolithique à l'émergence de l'État* (Paris: Fayard, 2003); Li Liu and Xincan Chen, *State Formation in Early China* (London: Duckworth, 2003); R. Thapar, *From Lineage to State* (New Delhi: Oxford University Press, 1984).

39   E. Cassin, *La Splendeur divine. Introduction à l'étude de la mentalité mésopotamienne* (Paris: Mouton, 1968).

40   H. Frankfort, *Kingship and the Gods: A Study of Ancient Near Eastern Religion as the Integration of Society and Nature*, preface S. N. Kramer (Chicago: University of Chicago Press, 1978 [1948]).

significant was imbedded in the life of the cosmos, and it was precisely the king's function to maintain the harmony of that integration.'[41]

To understand the importance at this time of the 'religious' relationship with nature and the polytheistic character of these religions, it must be remembered that the Nile Valley or the banks of the Euphrates and Tigris Rivers are regions where some intensive forms of agriculture and animal husbandry already had a long history. Rivers were also important avenues of communication and the transportation of material resources. Such development brought with it a steep growth in local population and the capacity to create surpluses for social groups – priests, craftsmen, warriors, tribal chiefs, et cetera – who no longer produced their own material means of subsistence and social existence.

Since the end of the Neolithic era, the populations of these regions had entered into a *new relationship with their natural environment.*[42] This was a relationship unknown to peoples who still subsisted from hunting, fishing and gathering, and whose 'religious' relations with the masters of the game and fish were mediated primarily by shamans' alliances with these spirits.

Alternatively, groups whose livelihood depended on increasingly more productive and complex forms of resources had become sedentarised and depended, for their reproduction, on the products of that portion of nature which they had 'domesticated' and which in turn depended on humans for its reproduction. But this new relationship with a domesticated nature was a 'high risk' venture. Too much or too little rain, and the crops could be devastated. The slightest epizootic event could decimate the herds. In short, these new relations men entertained with nature could be, successively, a source of abundance or of famine. During this time, the gods of rain, thunder, the sun, the moon and the winds multiplied. The Sumerians conceived and

---

41   Ibid., 3.
42   J.-P. Demoule, ed., *La révolution néolithique dans le monde* (Paris: CNRS, 2009).

worshipped more than 3,000 such divinities. It was the gods who could visit humans with abundance, but also with sickness and famine. Hence, the growing importance of rituals and forms of worship, together with the privileged status of those individuals and groups who conducted them.

But economies based on increasingly intensive forms of agriculture and animal husbandry favoured unequal production and accumulation of wealth within or between these societies; intensification of exchanges; and regional, and even international, trade; but also internal rivalries and external aggressions. The societies of this era were probably made up of tribes organised into chiefdoms or ethnically based tribal confederations, which meant that the chief of the dominant tribe in these confederations was the chief of chiefs, the paramount chief. Yet the greatest chief was not quite a god (yet).[43] It seems that in order for political and religious power to take the form of a king associated with a god or God himself, other social and material conditions needed to be present. Temples and ceremonial centres had to be built; priests, craftsmen and servants had to reside in them to serve the gods and offer them daily prayers and sacrifices. The chiefs and nobility of the tribal groups also had to live there, and have 'palaces' and fortresses built for themselves. In short, cities had to be created, and therefore, in order to exist, had to control the surrounding countryside and the arriving and departing trade routes. Thus, it was probably with the development of cities that the first states appeared and that one of the tribal confederations' great chiefs turned into a king, concentrating in his person part of the relations humans entertained with the gods and nature, but also command of the armies, protection of the poor and the weak (in other words the exercise of justice and equity, etc.).[44]

---

43   M. Godelier, *Les tribus dans l'Histoire et face aux États* (Paris: CNRS, 2010); and Godelier, *The Mental and the Material*, trans. M. Thom (London and New York: Verso, 1986), chap. 7, 'Estates, Castes and Classes', 227–244.

44   M. Van de Mieroop, *The Ancient Mesopotamian City* (Oxford: Oxford University Press, 2004 [1997]).

One of the oldest codes of law ever discovered, that promulgated by the Sumerian king Ur-Nammu, founder of the Third Dynasty of Ur, around 2050 BCE – in other words, at least 300 years before the code of the Babylonian king Hammurabi – stipulated that he would ensure that 'the orphan would not be preyed on by the rich, the widow by the powerful, the man with a sicle by the man with a mine' (mine: a silver coin worth sixty sicles). He promised to stamp out the 'predators' who appropriated for themselves the cattle of the members of the city, and so on. The prologue of the severely damaged tablet on which this code is engraved is very important, for at least two reasons. It tells us that the god (of the) Moon was the king of the city of Ur, and that the god had chosen Ur-Nammu to be his earthly representative to govern the cities of Sumer and Ur. So, the Sumerian king was not a god living among men, as was the Egyptian pharaoh; he was the man chosen by a god as his earthly representative to govern the city on his behalf. It was, therefore, the god who was master and owner of the city, its inhabitants and its resources, as in the case of the city of Assur, the city of the god Assur. We also know that once he became king, Ur-Nammu attacked the neighbouring state of Lagash, which was a threat to his kingdom. He conquered his enemies, captured the king of Lagash, Namhari, and had him put to death. With the help of his god, he had thus reestablished the sovereignty of Ur over its territory. He then promulgated the code of law from which I cited the above prescriptions. With each of these, a punishment or penalty was associated, often measured in silver coin.[45]

This example gives us a glimpse of the social importance, in such a society, of certain local groups' monopoly on access to the gods, from whom one expected justice, prosperity and victory over one's enemies. Furthermore, the monopoly of ritual functions was often completed by the monopoly on the use of armed violence, an outward-directed violence to either defend the city from enemies or to attack them, but one which could also be turned inwards against those tempted to oppose their own subordination. The example of

---

45   S. N. Kramer, *L'Histoire commence à Sumer* (Paris: Arthaud, 1957), 89–91.

post-Vedic India – whose population was divided into four major categories, the *varna*, which were in turn divided into castes (*jati*) and subcastes – speaks for itself, since the varna and the castes provided – and still provide – the society with its hierarchical organisation.[46] And at the top of society stood the Brahmins, the only ones empowered to make sacrifices to the gods and the ancestors, and who were in a certain manner gods among men. Brahmins shed the blood of sacrificed animals, but not human blood. It is the members of the second varna, the Kshatriya, the warriors, who did this at the command of the rajas, the sovereign heads of the hundreds of kingdoms into which the territory of India was divided before the arrival of the Mongols and Islam.

The rajas, or kings, however, were the only ones allowed to take part in certain sacrifices and rituals performed by the Brahmins. In their person, they provided the link between religious power, which consisted in the rigorous performance of the rites and sacrifices, and political power, which consisted largely in dominating the social order and protecting it from internal disarray and external aggression. But this distinction between religious and political powers is an analytical one and does not correspond, as Henri Frankfort and Radcliffe-Brown have told us, to the way members of these societies thought and acted.

Which prompts the following question: What roles did violence and consent play in the emergence and consolidation of the first forms of state, personified by what we call kings, who were considered at the time to be close to the gods and chosen by them, or as gods living among men? Violence and consent are not mutually exclusive; they combine with each other, temper each other, and complete each other in the exercise of a political-religious power in accordance with the context, and the social stakes and problems this context poses. Indeed, there is no such thing as a minority dominating the rest of a

---

46   L. Dumont, *Homo Hierarchicus: The Caste System and Its Implications*, complete revised English edition, trans. M. Sainsbury, L. Dumont and B. Gulati (Chicago: University of Chicago Press, 1970); Dumont, *La civilisation indienne et nous. Esquisse de sociologie comparée* (Paris: Armand Colin, 1967). Cf. Thapar, *From Lineage to State*.

society without the use of violence, even if this threat remains only potential. Furthermore, passive acceptance of a relation of subordination is a far cry from voluntary consent to this relation. I therefore posit that, in the historical processes leading to the appearance of the first forms of state and their 'kings', violence weighed less heavily than the shared belief that it was legitimate to serve those who, through their privileged relations with the invisible powers controlling the order of the cosmos and society, served the rest of humankind. In the bodies and persons of certain humans, there resided powers that served the 'interests' of all.

Was not the kha, the pharaoh's breath, supposed to animate all living beings down to the tiniest gnat, which therefore owed their life to him and existed only through him?[47] Therefore, all living things were *indebted to the pharaoh for their existence* and all human beings owed him not only total obedience, but also the products of their labour and their very life. Without the shared belief in the (for us, imaginary) mystic efficacy of the pharaoh's divine breath, it is hard to understand the longevity of the pharaohs' rule. It was through the representations of and the belief in this debt all humans owed to certain figures (kings and/or priests) that new social relations were crystallised and legitimised. These new relations led to ranking the members of these societies into dominant and dominated, into socially higher and lower castes or orders. And the more (for us) 'imaginary' the functions ensured by a social minority were, the more these functions were conceived of and experienced as essential to the reproduction of the universe and society, and the more those who ensured them were raised above the rest of the society and placed at its heart.

But not everything in the invisible benefits the kings showered on their society was merely 'imaginary' or 'illusory'. To go back to the example of the pharaoh – source of the life force of all beings, master

---

47 H. Frankfort, *Kingship and the Gods*, chap. 5: 'The King's Potency: The Ka' (61–78). 'The god is the Ka of the king. But the subjects say: My Ka belongs to the king; my Ka derives from the king; the king makes my Ka; the king is my Ka' (78).

of the earth and the waters – not everything was only imaginary and symbolic in this representation of a benevolent god and master of life. Had not the appearance of kingship and the forced unification of Lower and Upper Egypt been necessary in order for men to finally bring the course of the Nile under control and to regulate its flow, which each year carried the rich silt that made the banks cultivated by the peasants both 'black' and fertile? To be sure, religion with its rituals, and more than simply 'religion', was necessary if it was to contribute to the appearance of new forms of sovereignty of a minority of society over the rest, and was to propose as a model for the crystallisation of these new forms images of the gods and of humans' relations with these gods, who are also supposed to live in a society and are ranked in a 'pantheon'.

It is in just such a historical and mental setting that the 'labour' any society (ancient or modern) devotes to its reproduction *as a whole* – in the form of rituals, initiations, and so on – must have been transformed into additional labour, surplus labour, in the service of those who represented, more than others did, the whole society not only to the gods but to men as well. To the subordination and dependency of these other men would be added various forms of 'exploitation', necessary for the construction of temples, palaces and fortresses; for the daily provisioning of the temples with offerings to the gods, and for the maintenance of those who served the temples: priests, servants, craftsmen, et cetera; as well as for the provisioning of the palace household and the men-at-arms, to provide them with the 'signs' of their distinction – ornaments and valuables circulating among the 'dominant' of nearby or remote societies, but also weapons, and so on. But inevitably, as some humans rose up towards the gods or became gods themselves, others became dependant, subjugated and even enslaved, or, as in India, outcastes. These opposing social transformations were thus mutually linked and complementary.

I will end the analysis of the role of the imaginary and the symbolic in the emergence of various forms of state with the example of the birth of the kingdom of Yatenga in what is now Burkina Faso. This example shows how symbolic rituals and practices can produce a sort of consent in peoples that have been conquered by violence. These rituals feature in the coronation of a new king among the Mossi of Yatenga, as they are described and analysed, remarkably, by Michel Izard.

The Mossi are descendants of horsemen who, coming from the south, from Ghana, around the middle of the fifteenth century, conquered the peoples living in the White Volta River Basin. They subjected the native peoples, who even today are known as 'sons of the land' or 'people of the land'. But the latter continued to carry out the rituals associated with the land and farming. When a Mossi king dies, a new king is designated among the sons of the deceased sovereign. Only those Mossi descended from the former conquerors can designate the king.

Alone and dressed as a pauper, the designated king then begins a long coronation journey that brings him back, fifty days later, to the gate of the capital, where he makes a triumphal entry on horseback, a king's entry. Significantly, his trip takes him through all the formerly conquered village where the 'masters of the land' lived. The latter have him participate in the rituals addressed to the powers of the land and to the ancestors of the subjected populations. But beforehand, Michel Izard writes, the new king presents himself humbly to the representatives of the original occupants of the country to ask them to accept his authority, to grant him the legitimacy that can come only from the powers of the land. He makes them presents. He is humiliated, made to wait, mocked. No care is taken over his food or his lodging. Then, by including him in the performance of their rituals, the priests and heads of the native lineages cause the king to be recognised by their ancestors and by the 'Land' as one of their own, and they confer a legitimacy on his power of which the conquest had denied him full possession. But the recognition of the king is at the same time the recognition by the king of the legitimacy of the native powers. This twofold recognition also validates the exchange of the king's protection for labour and for part of the product of the native lands.

Mossi kingship, which had been inaugurated by armed violence, thus becomes a sacred institution. The king alone unifies, in his person, the community of the conquerors and the conquered. He alone takes responsibility for the unity of the two communities on a same territory in spite of their opposition. And in so doing, he represents, on a higher level, the entire new society. He, and no one else, is the state. Once he is king, his person becomes sacred, hence the prohibitions concerning the king and all those authorised to approach him. Even a power inaugurated through violence, therefore, in order to endure, needs to seek a form of consent from the conquered.[48]

---

48   M. Izard, 'Le Royaume du Yatenga', in R. Cresswell, ed., Éléments d'anthropologie, vol. 1 (Paris: Armand Colin, 1975), 216–258. And especially: Izard, *Gens de pouvoir, gens de la terre* and *L'Odyssée du pouvoir. Un royaume africain* (Paris: EHESS, 1992).

Conclusion: And so – What Is the Real?

From the foregoing, we see that the 'real' we experience is the product of the inextricable union of components that are at once material and mental (whether cognitive and verifiable, or purely imaginary), which, to varying degrees, enter into the production of the relations humans entertain with each other and with their natural environment. It is therefore impossible to mechanically oppose the real to the imaginary and the symbolic, for at least two reasons. The first is that nothing that is thought, made and enacted by humans can be thought without a symbolic support; therefore, the symbolic dimension is found in everything that is thought, produced and implemented by humans. The second is that a large portion of social reality is composed of *the imaginary that has been transformed into real social and material relations*. This imaginary as such disappears, not only because it has become a material and social reality, but above all because it appears as the presence of an aspect of the real – an invisible presence, to be sure, but one which we cannot help but believe exists, because it bears the meaning of the universe and of the status of humankind. This surreal real underpins everything; it is the place to which theologians and philosophers rush, as well as fortune-tellers, mediums and others boasting of privileged access to the invisible. Everything that is thought is thus imagined; but not everything that is imagined is imaginary. And that which is imaginary is either a virtual (or unreal) reality (play, art), or a surreal reality, but one which can then be transformed into social, material and symbolic realities (religions, but also political-religious systems).

It is now possible to enumerate and define the four activities that have gradually appeared as part of the work of the mind:

- The *first activity* is to make present to the conscious mind realities that are external or internal to individuals, among which is to think itself, when the mind seeks to understand how it functions. The realities present and presented to the conscious mind can be effective or imaginary, visible or invisible, material or mental, stem from perception or the emotions, et cetera.

- But – and this is a *second activity* of the mind – every representation is already an interpretation of the 'reality' represented. To interpret is to seek to understand the nature, origin and the operation or functioning of this represented 'reality'. In order to understand, we must begin by imagining. The mind is then faced with producing explanations, some of which are imagined but not imaginary (empirical or experimental deductions, logical or mathematical demonstrations), while others, on the contrary, are imaginary explanations that are nevertheless believed to be true. And since a representation never exists in isolation, it is always embedded in a system of representations that lends it meaning and possesses its own coherence, whatever the nature of this coherence. As soon as they arise in the mind, the 'realities' represented begin to exist, mentally, in the head of the person thinking them and therefore already begin to act on the thinker. In order for these representations to begin to exist socially and to affect others than those who thought them in the first place, their mental content, their 'burden of meaning', must be shared, that is to say, must be communicated to and be internalised by others, and above all be accepted as true.

- A *third activity* of the mind is to align our acts with our beliefs. This is not simply a moral issue, but goes deeper; it is a matter of producing relations between humans, and between humans and their natural environment, which give a social and material existence to those worlds imagined by the mind. And it is because these mental worlds are thought and experienced as 'true', or as 'more true' than others, that groups of humans invent the means to give them an existence outside the mind, to transform them into a way of thinking, acting, feeling and living – in short, into forms of society and social life. In this case, a mental world becomes the source of norms and dogmas that will prevail in this society. It becomes the internal armature of the social relations it brings into existence and that correspond to it. As a consequence, these new relations exist both *between* the individuals and the groups that make up this society, and *within* each of these individuals, in the form of rules of action, norms of conduct with which each person is supposed to comply if they are to go on being members of their society. And in complying, they reproduce the society which in turn produces them.

- Finally, *the last activity* of the mind is to produce value judgments – positive, negative or neutral – about the realities humans face, the actions they produce or undergo. For it is also value judgments that validate or invalidate the legitimacy of the order reigning in a society and which lead its members to accept or contest this order.

These four activities of the mind are complementary and work together to give *meaning* to the world around us, to others and to each of us; and in this sense they enable us to act consciously on the world, on others and on ourselves, and to react to what the world and others do to each of us. The strategic element in the exercise of the mind, and in humans' determination to create corresponding social relations among themselves, is therefore the question of what should be held to be 'true', the question of truth. This question is a universal condition of the exercise of thought and action. But we have seen that the mind can respond with two distinct logics. One logic distinguishes and opposes the possible and the impossible; the other holds that the impossible is possible, and therefore that it is not opposed to the possible but encompasses it.

The two logics are not mutually exclusive.[1] Someone can be a good blacksmith, who has mastered all the necessary technical gestures, and still invoke the god of fire when forging tools or weapons. Someone can become a great mathematician, like Descartes or Pascal, and still

---

1 M. Godelier, 'L'Impossible est possible. Réflexions sur les racines du Croire et des Croyances', in *D'une anthropologie du chamanisme vers une anthropologie du Croire. Hommage à l'oeuvre de Roberte Hamayon* (Paris: EPHE, 2013), 414–437.

believe that Jesus of Nazareth was the son of God and that the miracles he is said to have performed really happened: healing the blind, multiplying loaves of bread, walking on water, raising the dead, and so on. Yet the experimental sciences and the modern logical and mathematical sciences have had to rid their reasoning process of the thinking characteristic of the religious imaginary: namely, deductions based on anthropocentric representations that construct worlds which are at once like and unlike the world of humans.[2]

The human adventure began well before the appearance of our species, *Homo sapiens sapiens*. It had already begun when our ancestors came to have a brain that allowed them to imagine that which no longer was, or was not yet, or that which existed elsewhere than where they stood; a brain that also allowed them to relate events they had witnessed to other humans who had not been present; or conversely, to understand the account of events they themselves had not witnessed. Once their minds had become capable of imagining alternatives and a protolanguage had enabled them to communicate them, the crucial feature of humanity was already present in these humanities that preceded our own, or that lived alongside us for a long time. When construction workers discovered a burial site in a cave in the Atapuerca Mountains, near the Spanish town of Burgos, containing the bodies of thirty-two individuals of every age, they found that alongside one of them had been placed a magnificent red quartz biface. From this, archaeologists were able to deduce that these individuals, who were some 300,000 years old and belong to a species that probably preceded *Homo neanderthalensis*, had invented something like kinship relations (one does not bury enemies) and already imagined the existence of an afterlife, an invisible hereafter where the deceased continue to exist in another form and can take with them a favourite object, or one that continues to be of use to them.[3]

---

2   A. Piette, 'Quand croire c'est faire et un peu plus', in E. Aubin-Boltanski, A.-S. Lamine and N. Luca, eds, *Croire en actes* (Paris: L'Harmattan, 2014), 63–76. Also Piette, *Le fait religieux* (Paris: Economica, 2003).

3   M. Godelier, *The Metamorphoses of Kinship*, trans. N. Scott (London and New York: Verso, 2011), 552.

Let us remember what the young Marx had to say in 1845 about Feuerbach's work: 'Feuerbach starts out from the fact of religious self-alienation, the duplication of the world into a religious, imagined world and a real one. His work consists in the dissolution of the religious world into its secular basis. He overlooks the fact that after completing this work, the chief thing still remains to be done.'[4]

Marx did not tell us what the 'chief thing' remaining to be done was. Today we know that relations of production and their transformations cannot be the source of religious imaginaries, even if their transformations play a role in turning religious systems into power systems. The origin of religious imaginaries lies not in our capacity to live in society, but to produce societies in order to live and to legitimise their structures and their underlying order by referring to their 'truth', a 'truth' whose 'proofs' are often imaginary. Will humankind one day be able to stop inventing worlds that do not exist, in order to create worlds in which we will go on existing?

Andros, 3 July 2014

Paris, 21 May 2015

---

4   K. Marx, *Theses on Feuerbach*, from Frederick Engels, *Ludwig Feuerbach and the End of Classical German Philosophy* (Beijing: Foreign Languages Press, 1976), 61–62.

Bibliography

Adler, A., *Le Pouvoir et l'interdit. Royauté et religion en Afrique Noire*, Paris: Albin Michel, 2010.

Althabe, G., *Oppression et libération dans l'imaginaire*, Paris: Maspero, 1969.

Aristotle, *Organon*, vol. 3, *Les Premiers Analytiques*, Paris: Vrin, 1966.

Asimov, I., *Foundation and Empire*, New York: Bantam Spectra, 1991.

Assmann, J., *Maât, L'Égypte pharaonique et l'idée de justice sociale*, Paris: Julliard, 1989.

Augé, M., *Théorie des pouvoirs et idéologie*, Paris: Hermann, 1975.

Azria, R. and D. Hervieu-Léger, *Dictionnaire des faits religieux*, Paris: PUF, 2011.

Balandier, G., *Anthropologie politique*, Paris: PUF, 1967.

———, *La Vie quotidienne au Royaume de Kongo du XVI au XVIIIe siècles*, Paris: Hachette, 1965.

Bateson, G., *Mind and Nature: A Necessary Unity*, New York: Dutton, 1979.

Bazin, J., 'Genèse de l'État et formation d'un champ politique. Le Royaume de Segu', *Revue française de science politique* 38:5, 709–719.

Bloch, M., *Les Rois thaumaturges. Étude sur le caractère surnaturel prêté à la puissance royale particulièrement en France et en Angleterre*, Paris: Armand Colin, 1961 [1924].

Bottéro, J., *Mésopotamie. L'écriture, la raison et les dieux*, Paris: Gallimard, 1989.

———, *Naissance de Dieu, la Bible et l'historien*, Paris: Gallimard, 1986.

Boureau, A., 'Des politiques tirées de l'Écriture. Byzance et l'Occident', *Annales HSS*, (2000), 879–887.

Brown, P., *Society and the Holy in Late Antiquity*, Berkeley: University of California Press, 1982.

———, *The Cult of the Saints: Its Rise and Function in Latin Christianity*, Chicago: University of Chicago Press, 1981.

Cassin, E., *La Splendeur divine. Introduction à l'étude de la mentalité mésopotamienne*, Paris: Mouton, 1968.

Cassirer, E., *La Philosophie des formes symboliques*, 3 vols., Paris: Minuit, 1972.

Castoriadis, C., *L'Institution imaginaire de la société*, Paris: Seuil, 1975.

Caveing, M., *Le Problème des objets dans la pensée mathématique*, Paris: Vrin, 2004.

Childe, G., *La Naissance de la civilisation*, Paris: Gonthier, 1964.

Chomsky, N., *Language and Mind*, Cambridge: Cambridge University Press, 2006 [1968].

———, *Syntactic Structures*, The Hague: Mouton, 1957.

Claessen, H. and P. Skalnik, *The Early State*, The Hague: Mouton, 1978.

Clavel-Levêque, M., *L'Empire des jeux. Espace symbolique et pratique sociale dans le Monde Romain*, Paris and Lyon: CNRS, 1984.

Connelly, M., *Créance de sang*, Paris: Seuil, 2003.

Dagron, G., *Empereur et prêtre. Étude sur le 'césaro-papisme' byzantin*, Paris: Gallimard, 1996.

Dampierre, É., *Un royaume bandia du Haut-Oubangui*, Paris: Plon, 1967.

De Boysson-Bardies, B., *Comment la parole vient aux enfants*, Paris: Odile Jacob, 1996.

De Heusch, L., *Le Roi ivre ou l'origine de l'État*, Paris: Gallimard, 1972.

De Saussure, F., *Cours de linguistique générale*, Paris: Payot, 1972 [1916].

Demoule, J.-P., ed., *La Révolution néolithique dans le monde*, Paris: CNRS, 2009.

Détienne, M., *Tracés de foundation*, Paris: Leeuwen and Peeters, 1980.

Dianteill, E., 'Le pouvoir des objets. Culture matérielle et religion en Afrique et en Haïti', *Annales des sciences sociales des religions* 110 (2000), 29–40.

Dumont, L., *Homo Hierarchicus: The Caste System and Its Implications*, complete revised English edition, trans. M. Sainsbury, L. Dumont and B. Gulati, Chicago: University of Chicago Press, 1970; translated from the French *Homo hierarchicus. Essai sur le système des castes*, Paris: Gallimard, 1966.

——, *La Civilisation indienne et nous. Esquisse de sociologie comparée*, Paris: Armand Colin, 1967.

Duverger, C., *L'Origine des Aztèques*, Paris: Seuil, 1983.

Eco, U., *Le Signe*, Brussels: Labor, 1988.

Feuerbach, L., *Manifestes philosophiques. Textes choisis, 1839–1845*, trans. L. Althusser, Paris: PUF, 1960.

Firth, R., *Rank and Religion in Tikopia*, London: Allen & Unwin, 1970.

——, *Symbols: Public and Private*, London and Oxford: Allen & Unwin, 1973.

——, *The Work of the Gods in Tikopia*, London: Athlone, 1967.

——, *Tikopia Ritual and Belief*, Boston: Beacon Press, 1967.

Frankfort, H., *Kingship and the Gods: A Study of Ancient Near Eastern Religion as the Integration of Society and Nature*, preface S. N. Kramer, Chicago: University of Chicago Press, 1978 [1948].

Frankfort, H., J. A. Wilson and T. Jacobsen, *Before Philosophy*, Chicago: University of Chicago Press, 1946.

Geary, P., 'L'Humiliation des saints', *Annales ESC* 34:1 (1979).

Geertz, C., *The Interprétation of Cultures*, London: Hutchinson, 1973.

Gell, A., *Art and Agency: An Anthropological Theory*, Oxford: Clarendon Press, 1998.

——, 'The Technology of Enchantment and the Enchantment of Technology', in J. Coote and A. Shelton, eds, *Anthropology, Art and Aesthetics*, Oxford: Clarendon Press, 1992, 40–63.

Genet, J.-P., 'Légitimation religieuse et pouvoir dans l'Europe médiévale latine', in *Rome et l'État Moderne Européen*, Rome: École Française, 2007.

Godelier, M., *Communauté, société, culture*, Paris: CNRS, 2009.

——, *Les Tribus dans l'histoire et face aux États*, Paris: CNRS, 2010.

——, *Lévi-Strauss*, trans. N. Scott, London and New York: Verso, 2018; translated from the French *Lévi-Strauss*, Paris: Seuil, 2013.

——, 'L'impossible est possible. Réflexions sur les racines du Croire et des Croyances', in *D'une anthropologie du chamanisme vers une anthropologie du croire. Hommage à l'oeuvre de Roberte Hamayon*, Paris: EPHE, 2013, 414–437.

——, *Metamorphoses of Kinship*, trans. N. Scott, London and New York: Verso, 2012; translated from the French *Métamorphoses de la parenté*, Paris: Fayard, 2004.

——, *The Enigma of the Gift*, trans. N. Scott, Chicago: University of Chicago Press; Cambridge: Polity Press, 1998; translated from the French *L'Énigme du don*, Paris: Fayard, 1996.

——, *The Making of Great Men: Male Domination and Power among the New Guinea Baruya*, trans. R. Swyer, Cambridge: Cambridge University Press, 1986; translated from the French *La Production des grands homes. Pouvoir et domination masculine chez les Baruya de Nouvelle-Guinée*, Paris: Fayard, 1982.

——, *The Mental and the Material*, trans. M. Thom, London and New York: Verso, 1986; translated from the French *L'Idéel et le Matériel*, Paris: Fayard, 1984.

——, ed., *La Mort et ses au-delà*, Paris: CNRS, 2014.

Godelier, M. and J. Hassoun, eds, *Meurtre du père, Sacrifice de la sexualité. Approches anthropologiques et psychanalytiques*, Strasbourg: Arcanes, 1996.

Godelier, M. and M. Panoff, eds, *La Production du corps*, Paris: CNRS, 1998.

Granger, G. G., *La Théorie aristotélicienne de la science*, Paris: Aubier, 1976.

Grube, N., ed., *Mayas, una civilizacion milenaria*, Cologne: Könemann, 2000.

Hamayon, R., *Jouer. Une étude anthropologique*, Paris: La Découverte, 2012.

Harris, P. L., *The Work of the Imagination*, Oxford: Blackwell, 2000.

Harris, P. L., C. N. Johnson and K. S. Rosengren, eds, *Imagining the Impossible: Magical, Scientific and Religious Thinking in Children*, Cambridge: Cambridge University Press, 2000.

Hegel, G. W. F., *Faith and Knowledge: Kant, Jacobi, Fichte*, trans. W. Cerf and H. S. Harris, Albany: SUNY Press, 1977.

——, *Science of Logic*, trans. A. V. Miller, New York: Prometheus, 1991.

Hildegard of Bingen, *Scivias*, Mahwah, NJ: Paulist Press, 1990.

Hjelmslev, L., *Prolégomènes à une théorie du langage*, Paris: Minuit, 1968 [1943].

Huizinga, J., *Homo Ludens: A Study of the Play-Element in Culture*, London: Routledge & Kegan Paul, 1949 [1938].

Huot, J.-L., *Archéologie des peuples du Proche Orient*, 2 vols., Paris: Errance, 2004.

Husserl, E., *Ideas Pertaining to a Pure Phenomenology and to a Phenomenological Philosophy*, trans. F. Kersten, 2 vols., The Hague: Nijhoff, 1982 [1913].

Izard, M., *Gens de pouvoir, gens de la terre*, Paris: Editions de la Maison des Sciences de l'Homme; Cambridge: Cambridge University Press, 1985.

——, *L'Odyssée du pouvoi. Un royaume africain*, Paris: Éditions de l'EHESS, 1992.

——, 'Le Royaume du Yatenga', in R. Cresswell, ed., *Éléments d'anthropologie*, Paris: Armand Colin, 1975.

Izard, M. and P. Smith, *La Fonction symbolique*, Paris: Gallimard, 1979.

Jeudy-Ballini, M., 'Dédommager le désir. Le prix de l'émotion en Nouvelle-Bretagne', *Terrain* 32 (1999), 5–20.

Juillerat, B., *Penser l'imaginaire*, Lausanne: Payot, 2001.

Jung, C. G., *Psyche and Symbols*, New York: Doubleday, 1958.

Kant, E., *Religion within the Boundaries of Mere Reason*, trans. and ed. A. Wood, G. Di Giovanni, Cambridge: Cambridge University Press, 1998 [1793].

Kirch, P. V., *How Chiefs Became Kings: Divine Kingship and the Rise of Archaic States in Ancient Hawai'i*, Berkeley: University of California Press, 2010.

Kramer, S. N., *L'Histoire commence à Sumer*, Paris: Arthaud, 1957.

La Fayette, M.-M. de, *La Princesse de Clèves*, Paris: Gallimard, 2000 [1678].

Lacan, J., *Des noms du père*, Paris: Seuil, 2005.

Lakoff, G. and M. Johnson, *Metaphors We Live By*, Chicago: University of Chicago Press, 1980.

Le Goff, J., ed., *Histoire et imaginaire*, Paris: Poiesis, 1986.

——, 'La Genèse du miracle royal', in H. Atsma and A. Burguière, eds, *Marc Bloch Aujourd'hui. Histoire comparée et sciences sociales*, Paris: EHESS, 1990.

——, *The Birth of Purgatory*, Chicago: University of Chicago Press, 1986; translated by Arthur Goldhammer from the French *La Naissance du purgatoire*, Paris: Gallimard, 1981.

Le Goff, J., et al., *Le Sacre royal à l'époque de saint Louis d'après le manuscrit latin 1246 de la BnF*, Paris: Gallimard, 2001.

Le Roy Ladurie, E., ed., *Les Monarchies* (conference in Paris, 8–10 December 1981), Paris: PUF, 1986.

Leiris, M., *Phantom Africa*, trans. B. H. Edwards, Calcutta: Seagull Books, 2017 [1934].

Lemaire, A., *Naissance du monothéisme. Point de vue d'un historien*, Paris: Bayard, 2003.

——, *Prophètes et rois. Bible et Proche Orient*, Paris: Cerf, 2001.

Lévi-Strauss, C., *Introduction to the Work of Marcel Mauss*, trans. F. Baker, London: Routledge & Kegan Paul, 1987; translated from the French 'Introduction', in M. Mauss, *Sociologie et anthropologie*, Paris: Presses Universitaires de France, 1950.

——, *The Naked Man*, Mythologiques vol. 4, trans. J. and D. Weightman, Chicago: University of Chicago Press, 1981; translated from the French *L'Homme nu*, Paris: Plon, 1971.

——, *The Origin of Table Manners*, Mythologiques vol. 3, trans. J. and D. Weightman, Chicago: University of Chicago Press, 1990; translated from the French *L'Origine des manières de table*, Paris: Plon, 1968.

——, *The Raw and the Cooked: Introduction to a Science of Mythology*, Mythologiques vol. 1, trans. J. and D. Weightman, Harmondsworth: Penguin, 1986; translated from the French *Le Cru et le cuit*, Mythologiques vol. 1, Paris: Plon, 1964.

——, *The Savage Mind*, Chicago: University of Chicago Press, 1966; translated from the French *La Pensée sauvage*, Paris: Plon, 1962.

——, *The Way of the Masks*, trans. S. Modelski, Seattle: University of Washington Press, 1982; translated from the French *La Voie des masques*, Paris: Plon, 1975.

Lewis, B., *Le Langage politique de l'Islam*, Paris: Gallimard, 1988.

Li Liu and Xincan Chen, *State Formation in Early China*, London: Duckworth, 2003.

Malamoud, C., *Féminité de la parole. Études sur l'Inde Ancienne*, Paris: Albin Michel, 2005.

Malinowski, B., *Argonauts of the Western Pacific*, London: Routledge, 1922.

Marshal, G. P., 'Jalons pour une histoire de l'iconoclasme au Moyen Âge', *Annales, HSS* 5 (1995), 1135–1156.

Meek, D., *Les Dieux égyptiens*, Paris: Hachette, 1993.

Menu, B., 'La Mise en place des structures étatiques dans l'Égypte du IVe millénaire', *BIFAO* 103 (2003), 307–326.

——, *Maât. L'ordre juste du monde*, Paris: Éditions Michalon, 2005.

Métraux, A., *Les Incas*, Paris: Seuil, 1962.

M. Fortes and E. E. Evans-Pritchard, eds, *African Political Systems*, London: Oxford University Press, 1940.

Midant-Reynes, B., *Aux origines de l'Égypte. Du néolithique à l'émergence de l'État*, Paris: Fayard, 2003.

Pascal, B., *Pensées*, Paris: Flammarion, 1976.

Peirce, C. S., *Writings on Semiotics*, Chapel Hill: University of North Carolina Press, 1991.

Piaget, J., *The Construction of Reality in the Child*, London and New York: Routledge & Kegan Paul, 1999; translated from the French *La Construction du réel chez l'enfant*, Neuchâtel: Delachaux & Niestlé, 1937 [1926].

Piette, A., *Croire en actes*, Paris: L'Harmattan, 2014.

——, *Le Fait religieux*, Paris: Economica, 2003.

——, 'Quand croire c'est faire et un peu plus', in E. Aubin-Boltanski, A.-S. Lamine and N. Luca, eds, *Croire en actes*, Paris: L'Harmattan, 2014, 63–76.

'Plus réel que le réel, le symbolique', review in *MAUSS* 12:2 (1998) special issue.

Römer, T., *L'Invention de Dieu*, Paris: Seuil, 2014.

Rousseau, J.-J., *Profession of Faith of a Savoyard Vicar: A Search for Truth*, trans. O. Schreiner, Leopold Classic Library, 2016 [1889].

Sartre, J.-P., *The Imagination*, trans. K. Williford, D. Rudrauf, London: Routledge, 2012; translated from the French *L'Imagination*, Paris: PUF, 1936.

———, *The Imaginary: A Phenomenological Study of the Imagination*, London and New York: Routledge, 2004; translated from the French *L'Imaginaire. Psychologie phénoménologique de l'imagination*, Paris: Gallimard, 1940.

Sbalchiero, P., *Dictionnaire des miracles et de l'extraordinaire chrétien*, Paris: Fayard, 2002.

Scheid, J., *Les Dieux, l'État et l'individu*, Paris: Seuil, 2013.

———, *Quand faire c'est croire*, Paris: Aubier, 2005.

———, *Religion et piété à Rome*, Paris: La Découverte, 1985.

Scheid, J. and J. Svenbro, *La Tortue et la lyre. Dans l'atelier du mythe antique*, Paris: CNRS, 2014.

Scribner, R., ed., *Bilder und Bildersturm im Spätmittelalter und in der früher Neuzeit*, Wiesbaden: Harrassowitz, 1990, 46.

Serfati, M., *La Révolution symbolique. La constitution de l'écriture symbolique mathématique*, Paris: Pétra, 2005.

Soler, J., *L'Invention du monothéisme*, Paris: Éditions de Fallois, 2002.

———, *La Violence monothéiste*, Paris: Éditions de Fallois, 2008.

Soustelle, J., *La Vie quotidienne des Aztèques*, Paris: Hachette, 1955.

———, *L'Univers des Aztèques*, Paris: Hermann, 1979.

Sperber, D., *Le Symbolisme en général*, Paris: Hermann, 1975.

Tardits, C., *Le Royaume bamoum*, Paris: Armand Colin, 1980.

Tarot, C., *Le Symbolique et le sacré*, Paris: La Découverte, 2008.

Terray, E., *Une histoire du Royaume Abron du Gyaman*, Paris: Karthala, 1995.

Thapar, R., *From Lineage to State*, New Delhi: Oxford University Press, 1984.

Tolstoy, L., *War and Peace*, trans. R. Pevear and L. Volokhonsky, Vintage Classics, 2008.

Turner, V., *The Ritual Process: Structure and Anti-structure*, Chicago: Aldine, 1969.

Upton, A., *Charles XI and Swedish Absolutism*, Cambridge: Cambridge University Press, 1998.

Vaillant, G. C., *The Aztecs of Mexico*, New York: Penguin, 1950.

Van de Mieroop, M., *The Ancient Mesopotamian City*, Oxford: Oxford University Press, 2004 [1997].

Vernant, J. P., 'De la présentification de l'invisible à l'imitation de l'apparence', Paper given at the École du Louvre, 1983; republished in *Entre mythe et politique*, Paris: Seuil, 356–377.

Vernus, P., *Sagesses de l'Égypte pharaonique*, Paris: Actes Sud, 2010.

Wagner, R., *Symbols That Stand for Themselves*, Chicago: University of Chicago Press, 1996.

Weber, M., *The Protestant Ethic and the Spirit of Capitalism*, trans. T. Parsons, London and New York: Routledge, 2001 [1930].

Whitfield, J. T., W. H. Pako, J. Collinge and M. P. Alpers, 'Metaphysical Personhood and Traditional South Fore Mortuary Rites', unpublished manuscript.

———, 'Mortuary Rites of the South Fore and Kuru', *Philosophical Transactions of the Royal Society of London* (series B, Biological Sciences) 363 (2008), 3721–3724.

Winnicott, D. W., *Playing and Reality*, London and New York: Routledge, 1989 [1971].

Zubizarreta, V., *Traité de théologie dogmatique*, vol. 4, Vittoria, 1948.

Indexes

Terms and Concepts

Authors

Names

Societies and Places